Ruette,

God Bless -
And give you
Peace !

Pastor [signature]

# bitten

WHAT
DOESN'T
**KILL**
YOU
WILL
**PROMOTE**
YOU

## MARK VEGA

Print ISBN: 978-1-54398-497-2

eBook ISBN: 978-1-54398-498-9

# CONTENTS

# DEDICATION

This book is dedicated:

To my wife, Lisa - Your consecration to the Lord and dedication to me are impeccable.

To my Mother - Thank you for your determination and faithfulness in raising me and navigating through the storms until I reached God's mission for my life.

# INTRODUCTION

The cobra raises its head and begins to slither rapidly towards the Honey Badger. Suddenly, and with intensity, it latches on to its opponent and injects him with deadly venom. The badger backs off, losing his strength; the dose of deadly venom that now runs through his body is too much, and he can't resist it. The cobra moves around its victim as it does with all its prey. For three hours, it circles the dead badger. But what the cobra does not know is that while it's celebrating the supposed death of its victim, something is happening inside the badger's body. To understand what is happening, you must know something about the Honey Badger's nature. You see, throughout its life, it has plundered honeycombs to feed on honey, which means it has gone head to head with poisonous bees, frequently surviving attacks by swarms of them. These excruciating fights have prepared it for its encounter with the cobra. Every toxic sting this honey badger has endured during its lifetime, though painful, has caused its antibodies to strengthen, which has made the badger, for all intents and purposes, immortal in the face of venomous attacks. What was assigned to destroy him is the very thing that had made him invincible to such an attack.

The fact that we have a God-given purpose in life does not mean that our journey on this earth is without its struggles and stresses. Anyone who has enjoyed a life worth living has amassed their fair share of pain, tears, and scars. The enemy launches each attack with greater intensity, making us feel that we are in the last round and that the end is near. With every punch thrown and every blow landed against you, your loved ones, marriage, business or ministry, your strength and resistance are being weakened to a dangerous level. Paul finds himself bitten by a venomous viper, but instead of coming to his aid, those around him begin hating, judging and accusing him. As if that were not enough, they watch closely, expecting him to soon fall over dead from the fatal bite. Can you identify with this? People see a dangerous viper hanging from your hand, but instead of helping they begin diagnosing your situation. They make personal assessments as to why you "deserved" this venomous onslaught. In their eyes, this lethal viper will most certainly bring about your demise. There are vipers that have taken hold of us, and their poison has brought us almost to the brink of death. The most dangerous viper is the one that sneaks in with such subtlety that we are not even aware of the attack. Look at your enemies: insidiously dressed in black, celebrating your funeral. They are preparing your grave, choosing the flowers, shining your casket, inscribing your tombstone as they clandestinely prepare for your burial... But they have forgotten that God has injected you with an antidote that will neutralize even the most lethal of poisons sent to annihilate you...Through the person of the Holy Spirit, you receive immunity from Satan's fatal onslaughts. When the enemy comes in like a flood, the Spirit of God shall raise a standard against it. Now we can serve notice and boldly proclaim to the satanic kingdom and to our enemies: *Don't wait for me to die!*

# CHAPTER 1

# THE FOUR SEASONS OF WALKING WITH GOD

It is extremely important that every believer understand that his walk with God is made up of different seasons. There are those who do not understand this concept and later make permanent decisions based on temporary seasons (circumstances). Seasons like circumstances change. James the half-brother of Jesus tells us that if we submit ourselves to God and resist the devil, the devil will flee. The word used for flee in Greek is pheuxtetai, which means to *run in terror*. I submit to you that the devil also has seasons. He isn't always on the prowl, there are times when he flees. Regardless of the season you're going through—be it spiritual, emotional, physical, or financial—it won't last forever. Seasons change. The moment I became convinced of this, I felt compelled to make prayer an integral part of my decision-making process. Prayer is usually followed by waiting on the Lord's direction whatever that may be. I believe people who are under the misconception that their season won't change are oftentimes pressured to make a permanent decision about a temporary circumstance. The enemy (Satan) takes advantage of a believer's insecurity and uncertainty for "he is a double-minded man, unstable in all his ways" (James 1:8). It is impossible to define ourselves in our walk with Christ if we cannot discern where we are in life, or if we do not know where we are headed. "My people are destroyed for lack of knowledge" (Hos. 4:6). Ignorance destroys. There are believers who have lived under a cloud of self-condemnation for the last twenty years because of making wrong decisions that caused them great losses in life. Others are disillusioned because, though they did everything they were supposed to do, things turned out completely different than expected. The father of lies (Satan) then proceeds to bombard their minds with thoughts of condemnation and guilt, planting seeds of what could be decades of remorse and regret. Instead of progressing toward their destiny, they stop in their tracks and never love, hope or trust to full capacity for fear that they could repeat the cycle of despair again. Unfortunately in their latter years they are consumed by regrets and thoughts such as "Why didn't I . . .?" "Where would I have been today if . . .?" "What could I have done if . . .?" Thoughts of shame tend to dominate our minds and weaken our trust in God and ourselves. According to the Apostle Paul, Satan launches darts intended to infiltrate our minds and thought life. If he can control the mind, he can infect the motherboard, and once this is accomplished, the believer will begin to walk, think, and live bound to fear, guilt and shame.

If we are not aware of God's overall plan (some-times hidden) for our lives, it can cause us confusion and, in a subtle way, we suffer internal opposition.

At times, we misinterpret God's voice and the direction in which He wants to lead us. One of the ene-my's character traits is rebellion. He will do everything in his power to cause you to not heed to God's council and wisdom. It might be through the people he brings around you, or through relationship fall-outs, or spon-taneous strife with someone who serves as a portal of encouragement. You'll notice that the enemy will try to dry out any and every God-given relationship which has been a blessing to your life, so that you'll become more conditioned to "miss" God's leading. God, on the other hand, allows certain changes, losses, and failures to occur, which are necessary for a complete development of our character and His plan for our lives. It is essential to recognize the mission, plan, and calling that our God has for us. If we do not recognize His voice, we will never know what these plans are. It is indispensable to know who we are; whose we are; where we are. Obedience is laced throughout the bible because it is satan's kryptonite.

In its natural state, a diamond is simply a piece of coal. As such, it is something that lacks beauty or attractiveness. What transforms this stone into something desirable are the forces of heat and pressure that are applied to it from the outside. After many decades of extreme heat and pressure, a change occurs within the stone, changing its inner molecular structure. This metamorphosis occurs from the inside out, rather than from the outside in. The only requirement the coal needs to gain more value and elegance is resistance. If it can *withstand* the intensity of heat and pressure, then a total transformation occurs. But the moment the coal cracks, the process is ruined, and it will never attain its full potential. However, if it can resist, enduring the necessary process, the final product will be the most precious stone in the entire world: a diamond. The hideous appearance of the coal disappears completely, and what remains, in exchange, is its radiant beauty. The process, though lengthy, doesn't seem to be worth the wait or the sacrifice, but in the end, the result was well worth it. "But we have this treasure in earthen vessels, that the excellence of the power may be of God and not of us" (2 Corinthians 4:7). As believers, we are exposed to experiences of sadness, weeping, afflictions, anxieties, weaknesses, and fears. Despite these difficult moments, they are not a sign of defeat, but rather a process by which, if we endure, will result in change and victory. To reach the fullness of God's plan for us, resistance, perseverance, and tenacity are necessary. If you give up during the process, you will be disqualified and will be incapable of attaining God's plan for your life. God, our chief architect, allows certain oppositions and rivalries because He wants to design the characteristics of His people one person at a time: "We are hard-pressed on every side, yet not crushed; we are perplexed, but not in despair; persecuted, but not forsaken; struck down, but not destroyed" (2 Corinthians 4:8-9). The farther you want the arrow to fly, the greater the tension must be on the bowstring. The archer pulls until he can pull no farther, then he aims and finally releases the arrow. In the same way, God sometimes pulls us back as far as He can, aims us toward our target, and then releases us so we can carry out His purposes. Many times, we fight against it because we do not understand that we have been chosen for purposes so particular that only God can apply sufficient tension so that we can serve his optimal purpose and mission. We must allow God to do with us whatever He deems appropriate. If we are in His hands, we will not suffer any harm...Trust the process as you trust the processor!

## THE FOUR SEASONS

Born and raised in New York, I enjoyed the four seasons of the year - summer, fall, winter and spring. This cycle repeats itself every year without fail. As believers on our journey with God, we go through similar and important seasons. Summer is a beautiful time. The sun's heat covers the whole earth. The seas reveal their splendor and the trees produce their fruit. The leaves of the trees and the grass in the fields clothe themselves in beautiful color and magnificence. The contagious laughter of children can be heard as their joy spreads to others. During the summer months, daylight reigns for most of the twenty-four hours. The beaches and parks are frequented by people who enjoy their leisure. It is a time of relaxation, peace and joy. The environmental mood can be felt from person to person. The *summer* of a believer begins when we become a new creature (In Christ). We are in love with our Savior and has become our first love. Everything else, though necessary, is secondary. Our prayers seem to be heard and answered instantly. From the moment we open our eyes in the morning, we can feel God's overwhelming warmth. We see a real change in our character. Every time we read the Word we feel God's presence and we learn how to apply the scriptures to our own lives. This season is full of new experiences, from pleasant ones to unforgettable ones. Each passing day seems like a new lease on life. It is a time when God imparts new dreams to us with fresh vision. Our faith is optimized and our energy is revitalized. Every day that passes, there is a sense of fulfillment as we feel God's overwhelming love. This love spills over into every area of our lives. Grace and favor become new tenants in our journey with God. We are assigned two secret service agents to follow us wherever we go. Their names are goodness and mercy! We receive promotions at work that before seemed impossible. Every day we are thankful to be alive and our gratitude towards the Lord grows by the second. New relationships develop with our brothers and sisters in the faith. We are surrounded by kind, cordial and friendly people. These new experiences fill us with a security we have never felt before. God's fellowship and faithfulness have no equal. The love we receive from our social constituents seems unparalleled. More and more people take note of us each day, our notoriety increasing. We are sought after by new friends and our social life expands...popularity becomes a way of life as our Facebook friends increase and our Instagram followers multiply. Every social media post is "liked" and every status we post receives favorable comments. We have never felt so special and loved. We never want summer to end. The acceptance and notoriety can become intoxicating and smiling becomes the norm. The sun rises and until it sets, a constant stream of happiness overwhelms us. Joy is constant. "He who is of a merry heart has a continual feast" (Proverbs 15:15).

But after *summer* comes *fall*...changes that come in this season are without warning. Constant sunny days are now interrupted by frequent cloudy days. The grass loses its viridescence. The leaves change their color and fall from the trees, leaving them bare and devoid of their natural beauty. Clouds cover the sun, and with that, the beautiful experiences in the Lord begin to decrease. The friendships that were fostered during the summer begin to ebb. As the leaves variate, so does your social life. Moods begin to fluctuate within your circle, popularity begins to erode and your social life takes a turn for the worse. Your church family, along with your personal family, begins to fluctuate and you feel the tension with people you swore were your BFF's or your Ride or Die. Your prayers and petitions are no longer expediently answered as they had been during your *summer*. Autumn brings unexpected change whether you're ready or not which can be difficult to handle when you're in a rhythmic flow. It is important to know that you must walk this path by faith and not by sight.

Here comes *winter!* The season seems to worsen. Cold and darkness permeate, invading and taking over most of the day and night. The sun is hidden from our sight for most of the day. The trees lose their elegance and they no longer produce fruit. The grass dries up, no longer green but a dull brown. Nothing grows. All beauty has come to a halt! Everything becomes dark. When rainstorms come and snow falls, the weather turns dangerous. Highway accidents increase because of ice-covered streets, aka *black ice.* In the same way, in the spiritual life of the believer, God's promises seem to die. We notice that despite our labor and toil for the Lord, there is no optical evidence of growth or fruit. It is a season of testing. How will you react now that you don't have the same perks you had during the summer? It is a time when we must walk by pure faith and not by plain sight. We feel the loneliness that surrounds us, and at times it seems we are very far from our God. Like Jesus, the season of popularity has now become the season of opposition. Grace and favor seem to have dissipated along with the joy and notoriety. Welcome to the season of obscurity! But, take courage. It is in moments like these that we must follow God, no matter the cost. Although we may not see the solution to the immediate problem that is attacking us - the answer to our petitions, the healing of a sickness, the restoration of a marriage, the financial provision or the freedom from bondages, we can be still and trust in the God who is always faithful and all-powerful. In the dead of winter is where resolve is formed. Though people changed, circumstances wavered and God appeared to be silent, you were resilient enough to continue persevering and grinding through every obstacle. That resolve that formed in you is what I like to refer as "moxie" – the vigor, courage and pep that doesn't allow you to quit.

Job 30:26 says, "Yet when I hoped for good, evil came; when I looked for light, then came darkness." But be not dismayed, because spring has come!

The winter season was brutal, but thank God it just meant that spring was around the corner. Springtime is a time of restoration. Everything that winter took from us we now repossess. The earth begins to wake up from its long sleep. We see how the temperature changes. The sun shines with all its strength and its warm rays thaw any remaining ice. A time of new growth arrives, green foliage returns to the fields, fruits grow again; everything that seemed to have been lost is now recovered. God shows us His faithfulness. Newfound friendships and the replenishment and restoration of fractured relationships become prevalent. Even though we believed that God had abandoned us and forgotten all about us, we now see His seal of approval and a double portion of his goodness and mercy follow us every day of our lives. Our chronological time is redeemed, and our faith seems to increase.

Meteorologists confirm that the different seasons of the year are beneficial for the healthy development of our planet. In a spiritual sense, these seasons are also important and profitable for the perfection of our faith. Let us rest on the fact that as much as we'd like to bypass or skip certain seasons or their span, God has already established the duration of each and helps us to perfectly transition from one to the next. His timing is perfect!

# DISCUSSION QUESTIONS FOR CHAPTER 1

1. How long has it been since you last heard God's voice?

2. What do you think God has been trying to say to you?

3. Considering the process that a piece of coal must go through to be transformed into a diamond, does your situation discourage you or does the prospect of the final result encourage you?

4. What spiritual season of life do you think you're in? What reasons make you believe this? (Be specific and personal.) Knowing that seasons have constant cycles, how can you prepare for what is coming next?

# CHAPTER 2

# TAKE HEART

"And now I urge you to take heart, for there will be no loss of life among you, but only of the ship. For there stood by me this night an angel of the God to whom I belong and whom I serve, saying, 'Do not be afraid, Paul; you must be brought before Caesar; and indeed, God has granted you all those who sail with you.' Therefore, take heart, men, for I believe God that it will be just as it was told to me" (Acts 27:22-25). It is essential to know how important it is for God to keep His Word. When the heroes of the faith would become discouraged, they remembered God's promises. They understood that if God had declared it, He would fulfill it. God and His Word cannot be separated. As long as God has a Word and a purpose for a believer's life and that believer is seeking God and following the direction of the Holy Spirit, the Lord will protect him from death. We should fight in order to obtain God's promises because they are intended for our well-being. Paul instructed Timothy to fight to see the fulfillment of all those prophecies. Timothy understood that in order to receive that which God had promised him, he had to fight the good fight (1 Timothy 1:18). Perhaps you are asking yourself, why do I have to fight in order to obtain what God has already promised? There is an enemy whom Jesus described as a thief and a murderer. His sole intention is to steal, kill and destroy. Every promise, purpose and prophecy spoken over your life will be diabolically besieged in an attempt to kill what God has destined for your life. Every word that God speaks into your life will come to pass, but what determines its fulfillment will be your faith and obedience. In our country, faith has turned into a luxury, something that is not always necessary. In religious circles, the word faith has become a cliché, a simple saying. The prosperity in the United States has blinded believers. That is why many wonder: Is faith really a necessity when I have everything at my fingertips? The reality is that the more we depend on our material resources, the less we are going to exercise our faith, which will shipwreck God's promises for our lives. Storms are hurled at you by the enemy the moment God chooses you as His special vessel to use for His glory. In the Gospel of Mark, chapter 4, we read Jesus saying to his disciples: "Let us cross over to the other side" (v. 35). It is interesting to observe that the Bible says there were other boats; nevertheless, the only boat that was tossed about by the storm was the one Jesus had chosen from the rest, the one over which a prophetic word had been spoken. The boat destined to cross over to the other side, the one that was going to serve its purpose as a vehicle of fulfillment of what Jesus had declared prior, was being threatened by Satan. The disciples believed they were going to drown. I'm sure every shipwreck they had ever heard of crossed their minds. They were reminded of everyone they knew who had perished at sea. I'm sure that as thoughts of death gripped their minds, they panicked and became paralyzed. Perhaps you're going through a situation where the enemy has caused you to doubt your survival, whether you're haunted by thoughts of premature death and demise or of not surviving a current illness that you're battling. The enemy sends vivid reminders of relatives and friends who have died because of the same infirmity with which you have been diagnosed. Maybe you're staring eye to eye into the familiar face of failure and you are starting to fear that history will repeat itself...Fear Not!!! There is something you are forgetting...God's Plan!

They did not know the purpose Jesus had for them. They allowed the storm to dictate their faith. They woke up Jesus and the Lord immediately calmed the storm. But after the disciples had celebrated the master's miracle, they were rebuked for their lack of faith. Paul is also found doubting in a storm. The ship is breaking into pieces, as was Paul's faith. God, then, sends him an angel who informs him that it's necessary for him to appear before Caesar. Paul understood that his assignment was very much alive and that the call and purpose for which He had set Paul apart were still unaccomplished. At times, the current attack is so enormous that it overshadows God's future purpose for our lives. During those times, you need to lift your sights and see beyond the present and discern that what is happening all around you does not compare to what God will bring about in His perfect time. "For I consider that the sufferings of this present time are not worthy to be compared with the glory which shall be revealed in us" (Romans 8:18). Don't focus so much on what has happened. Whether storms, hurricanes, tsunamis, earthquakes or floods, look beyond the temporal. There is a permanent plan God wants to fulfill in and through your life. "While we do not look at the things which are seen, but at the things which are not seen. For the things which are seen are temporary, but the things which are not seen are eternal" (2 Corinthians 4:18).

The Bible tells us about a giant Philistine named Goliath, who caused great terror to God's people. God's promises and blessings for His chosen people, Israel, were being blocked because they had forgotten what God had promised them. Think of this amnesia as a dam that is sure to hinder the flow of blessings for you and yours. Instead of trusting in God, they preferred to depend more on their own strength against that menacing giant. God's purposes were paralyzed by a nine-foot giant. Israel, who had been called and chosen by God, was now being crippled by her lack of spiritual focus and remembrance. The people paid more attention to Goliath's countenance, physical appearance, the breadth of his shoulders, and his biceps and triceps. They trembled when they noticed the size of his bronze helmet, his coat of scale armor that weighed 125 pounds and the bronze greaves that covered his legs. The bronze javelin he carried between his shoulders weighed 15 pounds. His shield weighed so much that a man (his shield bearer) carried it in front of him.

When David heard that God's troops were being defied, he was not interested in Goliath's stature or his impressive, undefeated record. He knew that God's promises were far more powerful than the threats of his opponent. This strength and conviction came from his relationship with God. He was a young man who had an intimate relationship with the living God. From the time he was born to the time he squares off with the giant, David's testimony is perfect and his lifestyle is irreproachable before the Lord. As a result, God honors

His Word by empowering David and granting him the biggest upset in human history (even greater than Mike Tyson vs James "Buster" Douglas). The young man not only made a spectacle of the giant, but also caused a supernatural response when he dedicated his battle to God: "This day the LORD will hand you over to me, and I'll strike you down." It is important to never forget that when we exercise our faith, the storms and winds that are sent our way to harm us end up being useful instruments that God ultimately uses to glorify His name. "And we know that all things work together for good to those who love God, to those who are the called according to His purpose" (Romans 8:28). Do you love God? Does He occupy the throne of your heart? Does He take precedence in EVERY decision you make? If your answer to these questions is in the affirmative, congratulations! Every threat thrown at you will work in your favor. Be encouraged and trust in what God has promised you. Don't lose heart nor miss the plans He has set aside for you. Be encouraged and God will respond in His designated time. Even though the vessel that must carry Paul to his purposed assignment seems to be breaking apart into pieces, Paul takes heart! God has said that even if the vessel suffers loss, you and your loved ones will be protected until you reach the destiny He has for you.

Do not focus on temporal losses. Fix your eyes on eternal gains. In Matthew 13:24-30, we read what Jesus said about the parable of the wheat and the tares. Another parable He put forth to them, saying: "The kingdom of heaven is like a man who sowed good seed in his field; but while men slept, his enemy came and sowed tares among the wheat and went his way. But when the grain had sprouted and produced a crop, then the tares also appeared. So, the servants of the owner came and said to him, 'Sir, did you not sow good seed in your field? How then does it have tares?' He said to them, 'An enemy has done this.' The servants said to him, 'Do you want us then to go and gather them up?' But he said, 'No, lest while you gather up the tares you also uproot the wheat with them. Let both grow together until the harvest.'" At times, we pray asking God to remove the negative from our lives and undo every bad situation, tragedy, sickness or disaster. When we don't see the desired answer to our prayers we question God. Many have rebelled because they do not understand why the problems (tares) grew together with the blessings (wheat). Our human mind can only interpret the natural. For this reason, the Bible says: "The carnal mind cannot understand God." In Psalm 73, the psalmist is confused about not seeing the "wheat" of His faithfulness and instead only notices the "tares" of the wicked. He writes: "But as for me, my feet had almost stumbled; my steps had nearly slipped. For I was envious of the boastful, when I saw the prosperity of the wicked" (v. 2). The tares are always necessary so that the wheat grows. Pain and suffering fertilize our journey so that our destiny can blossom. How could we ever be victorious without conflicts? Opposing winds are imperative to achieving our goal and fulfilling our destiny. Joseph had to suffer in order to arrive at his final destiny. His brother's betrayal, the plot of Potiphar's wife and years in prison served as an incubator for his evolving destiny.

According to Genesis 45:5, everything was part of God's plan. The treatment David received from his brothers helped prepare his character and formed his courage and tenacity for decades to come and the hardships through which he would have to navigate God's people. Years of being ignored by his father, Jesse, despised by his older brother, Eliab, and harassed and hunted by his leader, Saul, served as a training ground for him to step up to the boxing ring to confront the oppressor Goliath. Hebrews 5:7–8 says, "[And Christ] who, in the days of His flesh, when He had offered up prayers and supplications, with vehement cries and tears to Him who was able to save Him from death, and was heard because of His godly fear, though He was a Son, yet He learned obedience by the things which He suffered." Even Jesus had to experience pain, sufferings, and anguish in order to learn to be obedient. I am convinced that God the Father used Jesus' disciples to develop patience and obedience during the days of His humanity. And even though He was the Son of God, while He lived as a human being, He had to deal with the "tares" of life. In the same way, God allows winds and storms to perfect us. My peace is in knowing that if I obey His Word and honor Him with my life, no matter how bad the situation is, He allows it in order to produce in me something that "normal situations" could never bring about. Romans 8:28 encourages us when it says that "And we know that all things work together for good to those who love God, to those who are the called according to His purpose."

# DISCUSSION QUESTIONS FOR CHAPTER 2

1.  Can you write down a promise made over your life that has yet to be fulfilled?

2.  What are some of the storms that have arisen to dim the destiny God has for you?

3.  In what way can you begin to fight in order to see that promise become a reality?

4.  What are some of the seeds the enemy has sown in the ground of your heart?

5.  In what areas can you thank God, even for the negative?

6.  How do you see the "tares" helping the "wheat" to grow?

7.  Explain in what areas your excitement has grown regarding fulfilling your purpose?

# CHAPTER 3

# DO YOU KNOW HOW TO LIGHT A FIRE?

"But when Paul had gathered a bundle of sticks and laid them on the fire . . ." (Acts 28:3) Already saved and fully living his faith, Paul encounters a dilemma. Having suffered the ravages of a shipwreck, he finds himself in the center of a vicious cold storm, where he has no choice but to embark on a deadly trek to safety. Now Paul knew that the only thing that could save him from the treacherous storm was a fire. He looks for sticks to start a fire. It is imperative that he gather brushwood and dry sticks to counterattack the inevitable conse-quence of pneumonia and/or death. He desperately needs to warm himself to escape the storm's devas-tating jaws. However, he faces a problem. "Dry" sticks in a storm? What was Paul thinking when he began to search for dry brush in the rain? Paul understood that in order to survive the storm without getting sick and possibly dying, he had to find dry sticks. Interestingly, Paul knew that God would come to his aid and provide him with what he needed (dry sticks). Nevertheless, we don't see him asking God to send fire from heaven as in the case of Elijah. Paul knows that his survival is predicated upon him *finding* dry firewood. It is good to know that God takes care of us, but He is not going to do for us what we have the power to do for ourselves. God's sovereignty (supreme being) and omnipotence (eternal power) should not be a deterrent for us to *seek* and *find* whatever the Lord is requiring of us at the moment. We must take serious responsibility for actions God expects us to carry out.

It is easy to confuse God's will for God's sovereignty. Because God allows something to happen does not mean he orchestrated it. 1 John 5:19 reminds us that though we are children of God the whole earth is under the control of the evil one. The enemy has capitalized on people believing that if God did not stop every historical atrocity and He allowed it, then it must have been His will. The Psalmist declared in Psalms 115:16, "the highest heavens belong to the Lord, but the earth he has given to mankind."children of God we are sanctioned God will never impose His will on humanity. We are in this world but not of it, meaning we have ambassadorship and are authoritative representatives of the kingdom of God. As we submit to our earthly authorities, we gain spiritual supremacy in the spirit world. Paul refuses to be confined by his limitations (neither what he sees nor what he hears) because he is fully aware that there is a spiritual kingdom of which he is a part of that supersedes the natural world surrounding him. I've seen so many believers confuse God's will and God's sovereignty. Oftentimes, the confused believe they're licensed to become idle and lazy in their quest to fulfill God's promises over their lives. All of God's promises require a certain level of maintenance. God gives them to you and provides you with the resources to carry them out, but their fulfillment depends on how you obey Him in the process. A photograph is developed in a dark room. The darker the room, the clearer the developing photo. But if light penetrates the room during the developing process, the whole procedure is damaged. God wants us to show Him that even in the dark we will trust His Word. No matter how dark the process is, we will never deviate from the goal. The widow of Zarephath only had a handful of wheat and a little oil, but after following the prophet's instructions, she was able to benefit from a miracle: there was an ongoing provision of wheat and oil according to her faith in the word given by the prophet through obedience, but she had to comply to his instructions and obey (see 1 Kings 17:13). God knows what needs to be cooked in every situation and will always share the recipe for a miracle. For Noah, it was wood and pegs (faith); for Moses, it was a staff (trust); for David, it was his harp and sling (bravery); for Samson, it was a donkey's jaw bone (security); for Gideon, it was a small group of three hundred men (fierceness); for Jesus, it was five loaves of bread and two fish (compassion).

If during the storm, Paul had let himself be guided by that with which he was physically confronted, he would've died, because finding dry sticks or anything else would have been impossible. Pastor Rod Parsley oftentimes says, "the proof of desire is in pursuit." Paul's frantic search for wood did not discourage him from his assignment. God always arranges to have the necessary components available to carry out His plan in us. As improbable as your specific situation may seem, there is an obscure miracle hidden with your name on it. Your miracle is suspended like a pendulum, subject to your faith and commitment, to see it come to pass. If God has given you a word, do not stop believing it. Continue to search for instructions to obey. Although everything may appear opposite of what you were promised, keep fighting, believing and expecting in that promise. Maybe your life hasn't panned out in the way you thought it would, maybe everything is a stark contrast to what He told you...do not faint...if you can believe it, you can have it. The health of your home, marriage, family, ministry and career does not depend on what happens to you in your daily life; rather it depends on how you respond to the vicissitudes of life. If you can believe it, you will hold it with your own hands. You must continue fighting to attain the miracle you're looking for, the healing you need, the complete freedom so desired, whether it be for yourself or for a loved one. If Paul had given up, there would be no epistles, sacred theology, church planters or even churches for that matter. I can picture Paul with a bad cough brought on by being exposed to merciless weather conditions, grinding, as he rejects fatigue and refuses to surrender to external influences. There is no doubt that at several points he was about to give up and die, but at that exact moment the Holy Spirit reminded him of the word God had given him before leaving on that trip: ". . .since not a hair will fall from the head of any of you" (Acts 27:34). Paul's steadfastness and desire led him to find what only God could have preserved for him during the torrential downpour...dry sticks!

If you want to conquer your storm, you will have to remember certain aspects of Paul's journey. 1) There are dry sticks hidden miraculously 2) You've got to use your faith to find what God has resourced you with during the storm 3) Warning: you will not find them at the beginning of your search and 4) Do not give up, take courage, keep digging, even though you are overcome with fatigue. I promise that you will soon reach what God has put in your path- the necessary resources to give you warmth, comfort, energy and light to guide you on to your destiny. During an evangelistic tour that my wife and I made in 1998 through Cuba, we found ourselves giving some marital conferences. In the corner of the classroom during one meeting sat a couple that had decided to succumb to the problematic situation that was destroying their marriage. The husband had the letter of divorce in his hand. For two years they had not found the "dry sticks" in the storm. Another couple had invited them to church; as a last attempt they decided to come. In that conference, they were able to find what had been there the entire time; *their* "dry sticks." They had not found it before because it was hidden and they had not searched. That afternoon, God intervened on behalf of that couple. They were able to forgive each other, and they found marital reconciliation and God's forgiveness. I know people who have been on the precipice of giving up, but at the midnight hour decided to search for what was hidden and found it just in time to thaw the love that once burned but had become frozen. Perhaps your doctor has diagnosed you with a life-threatening sickness; trade in your box of Kleenex for a shovel and start digging.

There are "dry sticks" close by that God has planted for you to find. Your miracle is a dig away...Keep digging! Dig your heels in and commit to see God break in on your behalf. Dig in God's Word, there's a verse for that! Dig in prayer, worship and align every word that comes out of your mouth with God's Word. Remember, the only things Satan can use against you are your words. Why? Because what comes out of our mouths is either going to align with God's Word or the devil's scheme for your life. Ask God for guidance and wisdom, and He will tell you where to dig deep. "Trust in the LORD with all your heart and lean not on your own understanding" (Proverbs 3:5). Just as God provided the impossible for Paul—the dry sticks in a hurricane—He will do the impossible for you as well. Everything is possible for him who believes! The fire represents the presence of the Lord, which is essential in our lives. The presence of God's Spirit fends off and protects against Satan's demise. The Word of God is the only book you will ever read in the presence of its author. That is significant because deep in the recesses of our soul and spirit should exist a conscientious reality that proclaims, I CAN DO ALL THINGS THROUGH JESUS CHRIST WHO STRENGTHENS ME!

Notice that Paul never asked anyone for help in finding what God had hidden for him. Neither did Abraham as his townsmen went to look for a ram to sacrifice, but boldly declared, when God told him to sacrifice his only son Isaac...The Lord will provide! When you decide to build a spiritual fire in your life, you cannot depend on others. You must know how to establish an intimate relationship with God. Primarily, God gives us a church where we can persevere in the faith, a pastor who shepherds us and a community of spiritual siblings that end up becoming closer to us than our biological families. Many people have lost faith in the church for various reasons. Wherever and whenever you have the human element, there will always exist the propensity of failure and letdowns. The beautiful dynamic of the church are the imperfect people who have the same commonalities, humanity, frailties, rejection, shame and guilt. Yet understand that we carry each other's healing. The apostle, James, wrote, "confess your sins one to another...that you may be healed." Whenever we gather together, be it our homes, coffee shops, or church, we sharpen each other, encourage one another and in a spirit of unity, we tap into each other's necessary giftings and become better together. People who attend church to worship God while not connecting with others are missing the entire purpose of the church. God never intended for us to be isolated from each other. Unfortunately, I presume these people only make it on Sundays or Easter. Jesus said, concerning the church, "and the gates of Hades shall not prevail against it" (Matthew 16:18). There are so many examples to my point, but I'll refer to the story of Paul and Silas. They began a "fire" in the jail where they were prisoners. They did not wait until they left to begin rejoicing and praising God. While they were still held as prisoners, they sang and worshipped Him. With their voices they began to pile "dry sticks" onto the fire. Picture them: they were in the depths of a putrid prison, surrounded by foul odors, filth, and even human waste. There, in the lowest part of what we can also call a dungeon, or a place of great mental and physical anguish, it was dark and cold. Undoubtedly, you could hear the shouts, the curses and the torture the prisoners suffered. It was an environment laden with terrible oppression and great loneliness. Nevertheless, Paul and Silas had a relationship so intimate with God that even with their feet in clamps, they began to pray and sing hymns to God with such force that suddenly an earthquake occurred that shook the jail, causing the doors to open and the chains to fall off their hands. Imagine the decibels their voices had to reach to overpower the rowdiness and vociferous insults coming from other inmates.

There is a big difference between a thermometer and a thermostat. A thermometer is passive and only reflects the environment. Although a room's temperature is uncomfortable, the thermometer cannot produce any change. It can only gage and reflect the atmosphere. In moments of despair, sometimes it's easy to be reflective and reactive, because it requires less energy. Some, by nature, have a passive mindset that I call thermometric. They are always reflecting the problems they are enduring. Their emotions and faith are controlled by whatever opposes them. In the book of Genesis, we see that Cain has a similar issue. He is not only wearing his emotions on his sleeve; he's wearing his heart on his face. You can see that his heart has rebelled, therefore his face is downcast. God recognizes the issue and takes it up with him. The all too familiar story unravels, and because his heart had hardened, not even God can make it pliable again. If Cain's mindset would have been thermostatic, he could have re-calibrated the temperature of his heart. Unlike a thermometer, a thermostat is aggressive and not only recognizes its environment, but also can bring about change to its surroundings. It refuses to be controlled by the temperature; instead it changes the climate by influencing the temperature. God wants you to change your situation.

Remember my friend, Jesus said you are the salt of the earth and the light of the world. Salt produces thirst. Imagine that, you have the ability to produce thirst in those around you in order to provoke a drink from the fountain that never runs dry...which is Jesus. Salt also serves to season and to preserve food. All this time we have believed that we obtained the job because God was blessing us. Although that may be true, I believe we are in the workplace, and classroom, and neighborhood because God saw fit to sprinkle a little salt for the sake of preserving and seasoning the lives surrounding us every day. Light rebukes and destroys darkness, and brings clarity to a room, illuminating everything. Perhaps your situation is dense, dark and cold. Raise the temperature on your thermostat! Don't let your circumstances determine spiritual climate. Open your mouth, clap your hands and glorify God because what is happening inside you is more powerful than what is happening around you. Hallelujah! I challenge you to begin a "fire" in your home, in your church, on your school campus, in your business or ministry. Wherever it is, seek God's presence - praise Him, worship Him, call out to Him, pray, sing hymns to Him. His presence is indelible and indispensable in your life. Take a few minutes now and prepare a place to invite God's presence. The key to a true experience in Christ is to seek Him while He can be found. His Word says: "Draw near to God and He will draw near to you" (James 4:8). Your intense pursuit for God's presence is flammable and will cause an inferno contaminating your entire spirit, soul and body...and even those close to you! I promise that if you make a great effort to light a fire for God in your life, you will be ablaze with the glory of God: "Therefore I remind you to stir up the gift of God which is in you" (2 Timothy 1:6). The gift translates to charisma in Greek. Notice it is God's gift, but to whom? To everyone around you. The process for spiritual maturity and growth is to endure the hard times, depend totally on the Lord and know that it's not personal, but that He's shaping and sharpening us as the very tools He will use in the lives of others. "Many are the afflictions of the righteous, but the Lord delivers him out of them all." (Psalm 34:19). "A broken and a contrite heart—These, O God, you will not despise" (Psalm 51:17). Our calling out to God moves Him: "Call to Me, and I will answer you" (Jeremiah 33:3), and He will do whatever is necessary to help you in your need. Paul understood that this fire was crucial for surviving the darkness of the night and for reaching his destiny. Paul was most likely facing all the necessary elements of pneumonia or some other sickness that could potentially kill him.

Do you know how to start a fire? Remember that this kind of fire is not a leisurely campfire where we relax and share s'mores while we 'kumbaya,' but rather critical in its purpose, which helped Paul to survive and dispel the sicknesses and dangers that were lurking. The Old Testament tells us the place where the burnt offering was made. There, the animal was tied to the wood. The quality of the wood determined the time it would take to consume the sacrifice. Good wood was used to keep the fire burning. It required a lot of work to look for and find good dry wood. Matches and candles won't do! We can become satisfied with the heat from "temporary" flames, and we do not recognize the benefit of continuing the search for "good wood." The duration of the fire depends on our effort to intensify the flames with dry wood. One moment of carelessness and the fire can go out. Just because you have some areas that are on fire in your life does not mean you have reached your goal. All of us have experienced moments of victory or of sporadic "flames" when we went to church or attended a religious event. Many times, we believe we have fulfilled that which was required of us, and now we can rest because we have succeeded in easing our conscience. We entertain ourselves with the idea that we don't have to continually pray, go to church regularly, or consecrate ourselves more because we've become familiar with past fires and know exactly how to start them. It is very easy to live on the successes and glories of the past. New levels bring new devils, which means the higher the altitude of glory to which God raises us, the colder it will get. Which will require special wood. The climate determines what kind of wood we need to start a blaze. It will have to be conducive to the frigidity surrounding us. I want to emphasize that it's not enough just to make a fire; the fire must be sustained for the duration of its need. Paul counsels Timothy: "Rekindle the fire that is in you." In other words, do not let it go out. Do not let the wood run out, because the fire needs to keep burning.

"And the fire on the altar shall be kept burning on it; it shall not be put out. And the priest shall burn wood on it every morning and lay the burnt offering in order on it; and he shall burn on it the fat of the peace offerings. A fire shall always be burning on the altar; it shall never go out" (Leviticus 6:12–13). It was crucial that the priest keep the altar burning with the fire required by God. When God informed Moses about the importance of the fire on the altar, He gave him meticulous details that He required from the priest. He instructed Moses on how to build an altar of incense, foreshadowing it with what would be expected of believers in the future that was to come. The altar is the believer's heart, and the wood represents everything that can be burnt. The more sacrificial your offering, the more pleasing it will be to God; and the more pleasing it is to God, the greater its intensity. All those things that cost you in surrendering to God voluntarily will always be incendiary. Those things that can be burnt up are the things that hurt when you surrender them to God. Everything you are going to sacrifice must be tied to the wood. The more it costs you, the more it will burn before God and the more pleasing it will be to the Lord.

Abraham tied up Isaac to sacrifice him. The valuable, pleasing, and incendiary sacrifices must be tied up. Six thousand years would have to pass before Paul gave similar instructions to Timothy, when he said: "Rekindle the fire (the gift) that is in you." To please God, Aaron and his sons had to burn the fat in the mornings. The pieces of fat were a symbol of sin. Everything that is not pleasing to God must be burned to attain the favor and mercy of Jehovah. Why couldn't they wait until the afternoon or the night to make this offering? Because the morning represents first fruits, the best of the best, priority and consecration. God is pleased when we give Him priority and give precedence to holiness, and do not postpone removing harmful and sinful things from our lives. Holiness is breaking allegiance with things that can potentially contaminate us. Our character, integrity, and personal life must be without "fat" or sin. If sin is not confessed and exposed to the flames, it will defile the altar and displease God. Though severe, these rules were for the benefit of God's people . I know the topic of sin is not a common one. Many pastors have eliminated the mention of sin to not offend. They have ostentatious buildings and large congregations, but the "fat" has thrived as well. My recommendation is to find a church that will tackle, in a spirit of reconciliation, the topic of sin. A church's goal should never be to attack sinners or the unchurched but to love them and lead them to the cross in a spirit of love. However, I'd also add, a church's goal should never be to make sinners or the unchurched comfortable in their sin.

Now allow me to get personal. Pause and evaluate your own altar (heart). Is the fire burning, or is there an abundance of "fat"? The Bible tells us: "Let us lay aside every weight, and the sin which so easily ensnares us" (Hebrew 12:1). Dear reader, you have the power to change your situation right now. The Bible also reminds us that "where sin abounded, grace abounded much more" (Romans 5:20). If you're guilty of letting the "fat" put out the flame of your altar, remember that God is willing to restore the fire. Simply ask sincerely and prepare yourself, because your life will change forever. Even though repentance (to change your mind) has a negative connotation, God has intended it as a means of forgiveness, peace and restoration. Don't procrastinate. "Call to Me, and I will answer you, and show you great and mighty things, which you do not know" (Jeremiah 33:3). In doing so, you will find rest for your life. Are you keeping the fire in your life burning high or low, or has it gone out? Whatever the case, I want to encourage you. Tell the Lord right now that you're not satisfied with the degree of your fire. Tell Him: "God, by the Holy Spirit, give me more of Your presence, more of Your fire, more of Your passion." I surrender all "fat" (confess those areas – be specific). Every act of sin confessed will serve as wood on the fire with your praise and worship. Begin to live the kind of life that produces in you the continual presence of the Lord. To keep the fire burning, you must leave mediocrity behind. There is more for your life. I know this as a fact because you're still alive. Let the naysayers snarl and doubt...the old is gone, the new has come. We are not ashamed of the gospel because it is the power of God for those that are saved! Escape the trap of worrying about the opinions of other people. Forget what they think of you and begin to look for the good "wood" to light the fire that will consume your life and bring hope to those around you...after all, not only was Paul's life spared but even the prisoners who were shipwrecked along with him.

# DISCUSSION QUESTIONS FOR CHAPTER 3

1. What does the fulfillment of God's promise in our lives depend on?

2. Can you name a recent storm and identify the "dry sticks" that were hidden?

3. What changes need to happen in order to start a fire in your life?

4. What do you have to do to keep your fire burning?

# CHAPTER 4

# BEWARE OF THE SNAKE!

...a viper came out because of the heat and fastened on his hand. So, when the natives saw the creature hanging from his hand, they said to one another, 'No doubt this man is a murderer, whom, though he has escaped the sea, yet justice does not allow to live.' (Acts 28:3b–4) CAUTION: If you enjoy feeling safe and covet nonviolent seasons, then close this book now, because this chapter is not for you. However, if you are not afraid to stir up the evil one, keep reading. While Paul looked for brushwood during the storm, he was safe and never in danger of being attacked by any of the wild animals on the isle of Malta, but as soon as he begins to warm himself by the fire, he is suddenly assailed by a venomous viper. Notice that the viper is provoked and irritated by the heat. While Paul was surrounded by the cold, damp, darkness, the viper was comfortable, as it had not felt threatened. Snakes are cold-blooded reptiles. They are relaxed and tranquil in cold environments. It is only when the viper feels the heat that it will become violent. It is essential for us to recognize and discern the periods when we are under attack. It is very easy for us to fall under the misconception that our spiritual lives are stable because we are void of an attack. The temptation to confuse stagnation with stability exists. If we don't define these concepts well, we are going to be deceived into thinking that we are "stable" because we are free of the enemy's onslaughts. Worse yet, we can subscribe to the idea that not being attacked indicates spiritual supremacy and some would call this being *stable,* but I call it being *stagnant*. Even Jesus disagrees with this philosophy. He said, "Blessed are you when people insult you, persecute you and falsely say all kinds of evil against you because of me" (Matthew 5:11). If you are not a threat to Satan's kingdom, his demonic forces will have no beef with you at all. But when you recognize that you must abandon the things that are religiously mundane in your life in order to experience intimacy with God, then and only then will you begin to experience attacks. The warmth (fire) and presence of the Holy Spirit in your life will cause diverse diabolic forces great discomfort. The fire of God in our lives will always provoke the vilest of attacks. If we are comfortable, living cold and/ or mediocre lives, the enemy will have no problem with us, as we pose no threat. An attack comes in distinct ways because the Bible tells us (1 Thes 5:23) that we are tricomatic (three-part) beings; 1) spirit, 2) soul, and 3) body. The enemy will attack every area of your life. You will experience attacks *Spiritually*, on your faith, your hope, your love, your peace. Your spiritual systems such as prayer, belief, word, giving, worship, etc. will take a hit. *Emotionally*, you will experience negative thoughts, shame, doubts, fears, anxiety, tensions and depression. *Physically*, sicknesses, neurological problems, appetite loss, ulcers, insomnia and abnormal tiredness might appear.

The viper meticulously attacks with a specific plan because his ultimate goal is to kill you and the legacy that will come from you. His violence against you is not natural because he knows that you are not natural. With God, you are supernatural, and nothing is impossible for you to accomplish. Whenever one determines to become disciplined to become ALL that God has destined for him/her, whether it's a better parent, a healthier person, a church planter, an entrepreneur, or to look more like Christ in their character, the viper will target you, launching his fangs and inducing you with his deadly venom. Note, however, your adversary is predictable. You can forecast and calculate his approach because it usually occurs in the form of a counterattack. As you enter a more intimate relationship with God, breaking every barrier of religiosity, aloofness and laziness, the enemy will certainly assign his agents (demons) to hinder your walk and try to extinguish your fire for God & those around you. The viper thinks that if he can kill you spiritually, emotionally or physically, he will destroy you and your legacy.

We are told in Matthew 4 that when Jesus had finished his fast, Satan was waiting for Him with three different temptations. After your greatest encounter and experience with God, the enemy comes to undo all that you received from God. Satan was waiting to tempt Jesus as he descended from his fast. However, scripture reminds us that, "God is faithful, who will not allow you to be tempted beyond what you are able, but with the temptation will also make the way of escape, that you may be able to bear it" (1 Corinthians 10:13). It isn't until you have experienced great breakthroughs and victories in your life that the most severe attacks come. In 1 Kings 18, God answered Elijah with fire to burn up the sacrifice, and the man of God slays the 450 prophets of Baal. When the news spread, Jezebel and Ahab threatened to kill him. Elijah, instead of confronting them, having the assurance that God had just backed him up with fire from heaven, begins to run away terrorized, and goes into the desert, cowering in fear and hides under a juniper tree. It is amazing to me that Elijah is in this predicament. His clothes and sandals have been stained by the blood of the slayed prophets, as evidence of God's faithfulness. His blood-stained garments are a clear reminder that God is faithful and just. Yet yesterday's reminder is eclipsed by tomorrow's fear! He makes a permanent decision (to run away) because of a temporary circumstance (Jezebel's threat). As you're reading this book, take notice of the triumphant stains you have on your spiritual armor. Every time you were ambushed and about to give up, the Lord showed up and gave you the victory...hasn't he always been faithful? But, like Elijah, for some odd reason you find yourself running in fear. By not confronting the viper, many have hidden in caves and under trees. God does not want you to run, but rather, to submit every angst and fear to Him, resist the devil so that he flees instead of you (see James 4:2). Remember, whenever you decide to make a heart change to live for God and make a difference, there will be venomous attacks along the way but always remind yourself that greater is He who is in you, than he who is against you.

Paul is so distracted by everything going on around him that he did not see the subtle snake; the viper comes out of the leaves without anyone noticing it. How does he do it? Because he blends in with his surroundings. He meticulously studies his victim before attacking. No wonder we are warned, "Be sober, be vigilant; because your adversary the devil walks about like a roaring lion, seeking whom he may devour" (1 Peter 5:8). As soon as he sees his opportunity, the viper slithers toward his victim to attack him. Without his intentions being detected, he fixes his eyes on the target (Paul's hand) to destroy him. "The thief does not come except to steal, and to kill, and to destroy" (John 10:10). If we knew how vulnerable we were, our dependency, devotion and fervor would intensify. Your life can change in an instant. At times, we drop our guard because we believe we are invincible. The biblical character, Job, went from blessing to blessing because God took notice of his lifestyle, giving him the reference of *faithful servant.* Immediately after Job receives this elite endorsement, he lost his ten children, cattle, earnings, friends, and even his wife's support. All his earthy possessions came crashing down...just like that, Job had lost it all. The enemy has a way of attacking without warning. Suddenly, car accidents, sicknesses, and catastrophes spontaneously and drastically change the lives of millions. There are people who were enjoying a secure, prosperous financial life, but because of a sickness that required hospitalization, in the blink of an eye, ended up in bankruptcy. Satan is devoted to launching unprompted attacks that no one expects, causing great damage. It is said, in the world of boxing, that the most effective blow is the one the opponent is not expecting.

Paul is finally warming up by the fire when suddenly...when he is close enough, the viper latches onto Paul's hand. He instantly agonizes as he feels the fangs ripping through his flesh. As he anguishes, he receives a dose of venom that causes him excruciating pain. Interestingly, the people who are near when he is bitten hear him cry out and see the viper hanging from his hand, but oddly refuse to offer him help. Perhaps Paul was hoping that Luke, the physician, would give him first aid, or one of his friends in the ministry would pray for him, or that someone would grab the viper by the neck and kill it. But nothing of the sort ever happens. As if the audience's lack of compassion and proactivity weren't the worst, they begin to accuse and condemn him, hoping that he would die...can you imagine that?

Unfortunately, it is often at this juncture in life where many put their trust and hope in people, only to be disappointed to the point of giving up altogether, because of the immense offense. Many of those who have persevered in the faith have gone astray because no one helped them in their time of need. The devil has deceived them, causing them to doubt and entertain uncertainties in their mind. He has whispered: "No one loves you. Nobody cares about your need." He lies to them, making them believe that their lives have no value, or that they aren't important. The enemy frequently launches these snares at you immediately after you are attacked. Your adversary somehow knows when you are most vulnerable. Paul now finds himself going through a time of emotional uncertainty. There's no doubt that the devil is whispering to him: "Where is your help? Where is your God? Where is the God you serve? Who lets his servant die in disgrace in front of everyone?" I can picture the devil laughing at Paul and joining the audience of accusers who are slandering him, hoping his demise is near.

Undoubtedly, Paul is feeling physical pain, emotional loneliness and spiritual abandonment, while the five-pound viper, whose bite is fatal, is hanging from his hand. Sometimes, when we are going through a time of extreme depression, the fact that no one reaches out to offer help wounds us more than the attack itself. Especially those who we "expected" to rescue us. The pain caused by rejection penetrates deep into the soul, where only God can heal. Paul raises his eyes and looks around. He sees that his friends aren't doing anything to help him. Not one person is attempting to deliver him from the horrendous experience. And that was the least of what occurred. Listen to what the people then began to say: "This man is a murderer. It's okay that this happened to him. He brought it upon himself." That sounds like a death sentence to Paul. Have you ever gone through a bad experience believing that some-one was going to assist you, but instead of offering you a helping hand, they offered a slanderous word to judge you? Have you ever been the subject of intense gossip, all the while knowing you were innocent? Have you been faithful to God, lived by example, lived above reproach? Are you a good father, a good mother, a model citizen, an honest worker? Jesus sympathized with Paul, and He sympathizes with you. The Son of God, who was innocent, never hurt anyone; neverthe-less, he was the object of many abuses. His enemies, who wanted to see him dead, mocked Him and judged Him unfairly. He never defended himself nor opened His mouth. He knew that God would come to His defense at the right time. In the same way, Paul neither defends nor justifies himself. Instead, he prefers that God be his witness. He chooses to put his full trust and depen-dence on the person and power of the Holy Spirit.

Paul's example should teach us that when we go through times of criticism, gossip, and accusations, we should remember that Jesus is always interceding for us. He is our lawyer; he pleads our case and defends us from all accusation. If you find yourself defenseless and going through moments when no one is running to your defense when you most need support, trust in the Lord and in the power of His Word. God will help you, no matter what your need is. Don't rush to defend yourself. Allow the Holy Spirit to do that for you. I encourage you to trust in Christ and in His Word. If you are faithful to Him, He will always be faithful to you... and even when we are faithless, He still remains faithful (2 Timothy 2:13). Our God is a present help in time of need (Psalm 46:1). Your help is on the way! I'm a firm believer that many have succumbed to defeat because they didn't wait long enough for God to show up on their behalf. According to Isaiah 31, waiting on the Lord is tiresome, but those who do wait and cross the threshold of fatigue, receive renewed strength and are revitalized as their reward. Many have lost their faith, looking for a solution to their problems in their own power. Their wounds have caused them much pain, mostly because they were not aware of the faithfulness and justice of God. Consequently, their situation worsened. Don't take vengeance into your own hands, even when you believe you have a justifiable reason: it doesn't mean you have a biblical right. Let God be the One who defends you. Satan wants to blind us regarding God's righteousness and justice. If we acknowledge that God is always on our side, watching and taking care of us, He will give us peace and rest in the middle of the storm. Paul teaches us the importance of being guided by the Spirit and not by the flesh. It says in Galatians 5:17: "For the flesh lusts against the Spirit, and the Spirit against the flesh; and these are contrary to one another, so that you do not do the things that you wish." The devil uses the impulsivity and weaknesses of your flesh to bring despair and anxiety into your life. Many people, when they don't see a way out, drown in their own desperation. These same people, because of their constant propensity to be vulnerable to their adversaries, walk around life like sitting ducks waiting to be sniped. They act imprudently when they don't see a way out. It is sad when people with brilliant futures decide to end their life in an effort to escape anguish and pain. I'm sure Paul's carnal nature was telling him: "You are going to die, and nobody will care. God's promises are never going to be fulfilled in your life." But, on the other hand, his spirit was telling him: "You can do all things through Christ who strengthens you."

As believers, we must discipline our flesh to learn to submit to the Spirit. Years after, Paul himself wrote to the Philippians: "Finally, brethren, whatever things are true, whatever things are noble, whatever things are just, whatever things are pure, whatever things are lovely, whatever things are of good report, if there is any virtue and if there is anything praiseworthy— meditate on these things" (Philippians 4:8). Jesus said: "the flesh is weak, but the spirit is willing" (Matthew 26:41). We must take captive every thought to make it obedient to Christ. Like Paul, we must refuse to give up and instead fight the good fight of faith. Paul avoids death and defeat by focusing, concentrating, and ignoring the enemy's threats. The most surprising thing is that the inhabitants from the island are the ones who initiate the verbal attack against Paul when they see the viper hanging from his hand. They believe that the serpent was an indication of the kind of person that Paul was. There are those who believe that an integral follower cannot be attacked by the devil. The Bible tells us about men and women whom God used mightily, but they went through the crucible of affliction and injustice. Our spiritual position does not exempt us from Satan's attacks or problems. In fact, the more we seek to be a life-long disciple of Christ, the more we are going to stir up Satan's kingdom. We will never see someone attacking a vagabond, but we have seen assassinations of well-known politicians who have made a difference.

Walking uprightly and determining to make a difference will incite attacks and storms in our lives. The Bible tells us about Joseph, who was sold as a slave. He was treated unfairly, locked up in a jail and suffered immensely for being a righteous man. In the same manner, Job lost everything just for being a righteous man before God. Being honest, righteous, and noble has its price. Are you willing to pay the price? If Joseph had let himself be seduced by Potiphar's wife, he would not have gone through all he went through, but he knew a secret...that sin has a way of finding you and making you pay with interest. Because Joseph kept his faith and dignity, he fled from her sexual advances and had to spend seven years in jail; however, in the end he was vindicated and exalted as Pharaoh's right-hand man. Even though he was sold into slavery by his brothers, he recognized God's hand at work in his life. Later, he tells his brothers, who had sold him: "But now, do not therefore be grieved or angry with yourselves because you sold me here; for God sent me before you to preserve life." When Joseph's brothers come to Egypt to buy wheat, Joseph ponders over all his past experiences and ends up saying: "God sent me." You may find yourself reading this book, and you still do not understand why you have been the victim of so many negative occurrences. Let me encourage you by saying: "God sent you." He wants you to hand him the controls of your life. The sovereignty of God is our peace. I have never taken an antidepressant or a "relaxer" to calm my nerves. When I think about God's sovereignty, I can lay my head on His sovereign lap and know that He will embrace me because He loves me, and it is going to be fine because He has control over everything: "...casting all your care upon Him, for He cares for you" (1 Peter 5:7).

# SHAKE YOURSELF

With intense pain in his soul and his body, Paul violently shakes the viper. At some point we will have to decide what we are going to do with the viper. We have two options: The first option we have is to treat the viper with a lot of fear and respect, asking it to let go of us and leave, and hope that it does. At times, fear can hinder us and keep us from operating at our maximum capacity. We perceive the enemy and his attacks as being greater than they really are. We yield to the attacker, simply because we are terrified of a confrontation. Many avoid confrontation at all costs. Thousands of people have suffered abuse at the hands of a family member or loved one, and because of the fear, shame, and even feelings of guilt, many have been held captive by their own self-imposed prison because they prefer to suffer silently in torment for the rest of their lives. For many, it's easier to suffer the ill effects than to confront the issue at hand. That's why so many choose to sacrifice themselves, rather than face the truth and bring resolution to the circumstance, even though the process might be tedious and uncomfortable. It's the reason millions continue living a nightmare instead of allowing God to set them free. The devil lies to them, telling them that if they open their mouths to free themselves from the viper, they are going to suffer severe repercussions. These threats have trapped multitudes of people throughout the world and even within our own churches. There are people who, on the outside, seem to be living lives of freedom and enjoying a fulfilled life, but inwardly, they are living behind the bars of terrifying experiences. Freedom has never been obtained passively...Freedom demands a price. Your freedom has already been paid for by Jesus Christ, as he took our place on that old rugged cross, the death sentence had our name on it but he paid the price for our sake. Accept all that Jesus offers today and you will begin the first steps to walking in freedom, true freedom! If you're only living and tolerating your situation, you will never confront it. You are only experiencing what you have allowed to come into your life. The only way we are going to receive deliverance is by confessing our wounds and their pain, and then allowing God to heal us. If we consider ourselves victims or sinners, 1 John 1:9 tells us: "If we confess our sins, He is faithful and just to forgive us our sins and cleanse us from all unrighteousness." The pain comes in different degrees and affects different areas in a person's life. We are susceptible spiritually, physically, emotionally, in our marriage, profession or ministry, but the prescription is still the same: an encounter with God.

The other option we have is to kill the viper by shaking it off into the fire, which signifies handing our pain, traumas, and bad experiences over to God. Paul chooses the latter. He decides to shake off the viper into the fire. It is important for us not to believe that, just because we read a self-help book, everything is going to be fine. We tend to believe that if we focus on improving ourselves physically that we'll remedy the issue. Not that any of this is wrong or unhealthy, but we need to understand that we are fully engaged in what the Bible refers to as spiritual warfare. Joining a church is indispensable because there you'll meet what Jesus called our real family, having the opportunity to serve others going through similar situations. Learning to pray and studying the Word of God have proven to be the greatest exercises I've ever been taught. It's worth noting that the viper didn't die until it was thrown into the fire. The fire completely consumed it. Let God consume what has latched onto you that you haven't been able to shake off.

Let's Pray. Father, I take control of my life in the name of Jesus. I shake off this viper that has fastened itself onto me and that has clung to my life to kill me. By the power of the Holy Spirit, I loose myself from the pain, the abuse, and the fear. Even though no one has come to help me, I surrender my life to you, and I also renounce everything that has kept me bound to the past. In the powerful name of Jesus Christ...Amen.

If your fire is still lit, you can be sure that the snake will not return to your life. Shaking means movement.

There should be movement and action in your spiritual life. If Paul had remained still, the viper would have killed him. There's danger when a person is inactive in their faith. The devil's plan is to immobilize you to the point that you are not alert to the things of the Lord. When you get up in the morning with no desire to live, depression and anguish come and try to make habitation in your heart. We must keep moving forward in the Lord. Let us continue to pray daily, and allow God to use our gifts at the church we serve. It is vital to maintain a strong discipline to study and apply God's Word on a consistent basis. Just because the viper dies doesn't mean that its effects died. The viper hanging from Paul's hand has been shaken into the fire. The viper is dead.

But I must warn you, however, not to be quick to celebrate...

It's true the viper is dead, but the venom remained in Paul's body. At times, we believe that just because the attack ceases, the effects of the attack die. Just because we don't have contact with the assailant, because he died or moved to another city, we believe we can rest, and everything will return to normal. It's amazing that there are people who are not careful about their lives just because they see that the attack has stopped. When we go to a doctor's appointment for an infection, the doctor prescribes us a medication.

And when we leave his office, he stresses the importance of taking the medicine before our follow up visit. But if you are like me, we often take the medicine only until we feel better. As soon as we stop feeling the effects of the infection, we forget about the medicine and the instructions of the doctor. Perhaps this example is comical, but the truth is we cannot adopt the same attitude with our spiritual life. Every attack has its effects. Satan also scatters seed, hoping that in due time it will produce fruit. There are a number of believers who sit in the pews of their churches each week, singing hymns and listening to powerful messages, but who continue to suffer from deep wounds in their souls because of a trauma that occurred years earlier. Although they are religious people, they are also acrimonious. They are victims of resentment, pain, and bitterness, which keep their wounds open. If they do not let God deal with their situation, they will continue to live tormented and inconsistent lives. Though the cause of the trauma ended years ago, they are still influenced by the side effects of the wound that never healed. The problem is that these infected wounds grow and run rampant through their emotions. While you're reading this book, I'm asking God to reveal these open wounds to you by His Holy Spirit, so that you can confess and renounce them once and for all. The hand of God is on your life to heal you.

# FORGIVENESS

Many years can go by before someone is healed of their wounds and pain. The easiest thing to do is to ignore these harmful emotions and suppress them in the deepest recesses of your memory. When you do this, the pain is then often not dealt with until one reaches a more mature age, such as thirty, forty, or fifty. Before you realize it, you've been robbed of decades of your life. The past infects the present and destroys the future. It is when you decide to forgive those responsible for your pain that you will no longer be a prisoner to them. Anger is like an umbilical cord that keeps you connected to your past. If you hold on to your anger, you will remain bound to the one who abused you, and that same person will control your life. Forgiveness does not necessarily free the person who abused you, but it certainly frees you. Forgiveness is for your own benefit. It's time to stop living in prisons of anger and bitterness that control your mind, emotions, and future. Forgiveness is the medicine a victim needs. If you do not take care of your past, it will turn into a cancer and infect your future. In Greek, forgiveness means "breathe out, exhale" (remove from your system). This does not happen automatically; it's a process. Humanly speaking, it is a very difficult thing, but God will give you the necessary strength to forgive. It requires a lot of energy to keep hate and bitterness alive. Anger, resentment, and bitterness can harass you severely, almost as if the abuser were still alive abusing you. You will be forced to rehearse the incident over and over again. This dilemma, along with what has been instilled in us from childhood, "What happens at home, Stays at home", is the formula for destruction, unless we seek the freedom that is offered in the name of Jesus.

Let's Pray. Father, I come wounded and traumatized. I need your healing balm. I believe the blood of Christ heals me and restores me. I renounce and forgive those who opened the door so that the enemy could use this against me (be specific; name each area). I accept your righteousness, and I am justified by your grace. I will never let this bind me again. Forgive me for not embracing your grace and mercy. The blood of Christ cleanses, forgives, heals and justifies me in the name of Jesus and by the power of your Word. Thank you, Father. Amen.

# DISCUSSION QUESTIONS FOR CHAPTER 4

1. How can you relate to the terms "stuck" and "stability?"

2. In what ways are you a threat to the kingdom of darkness?

3. How can you shake off the viper and kill it?

4. How much has your past infected your future?

5. Name one or more people you know you need to forgive.

6. Explain the venom in your life and the way it is affecting you.

7. What have you learned about forgiveness?

# CHAPTER 5

# CAUTION: THIS SNAKE IS VENOMOUS

*However, they were expecting that he would swell up or suddenly fall dead* (Acts 28:6). This was an attack like no other! When Satan discovers your potential, he launches his attack to destroy the destiny designed by God for your life. The attacks you face often are an indication of the calling or purpose God has ordained for you. If you make a comparison among people, you will notice that not all are attacked equally. In case you haven't noticed, those who are used of God greatly are those who, beginning with their childhood, suffered major traumas in their lives. Similarly, you can ask any ordinary person, who has been coasting for most of their life, and they will tell you that their life has been very normal and absent of any real storms. The more you pose a threat to the kingdom of darkness, the more attacks he will launch against you, with the purpose of causing you to pull back in fear or become discouraged in your spiritual journey. The enemy will use anyone and everyone to distract you and cause you to deviate from your true God-given purpose in life. He will use the people who are closest to you to discourage you from answering your call (aka your life's assignment). The devil is known for his subtle schematics and provocative traps. Whenever I witness a person decide to make Jesus Christ the Lord of their lives, I rejoice with them but also take the opportunity to warn them of the impending attacks that will come their way. The Apostle Paul calls this, "spiritual warfare." You can expect betrayal from family and friends. Finances are usually targeted and anything else that you placed your trust in before your conversion to Christ. According to Paul, there is a certain armor you and I MUST wear to survive the onslaught of hell. He writes in the Book of Ephesians, Chapter 6, regarding the function and importance of every battle garb suggested. Interestingly, the armor described protects and shields specific parts of your body such as your mind and your heart...*For our struggle is not against flesh and blood, but against the rulers, against the authorities, against the powers of this dark world and against the spiritual forces of evil in the heavenly realms. Therefore put on the full armor of God, so that when the day of evil comes, you may be able to stand your ground, and after you have done everything, to stand. Stand firm then, with the belt of truth buckled around your waist, with the breastplate of righteousness in place, and with your feet fitted with the readiness that comes from the gospel of peace. In addition to all this, take up the shield of faith, with which you can extinguish all the flaming arrows of the evil one. Take the helmet of salvation and the sword of the Spirit, which is the word of God.* - Ephesians 6:12

In another passage of scripture, Paul compares us to jars of clay. Several thousand years before he writes this, the Prophet Jeremiah stated the exact same thing. The prophet referred to God as the potter and us as the clay. It's amazing how, even though we are considered clay jars, Paul adds to this analogy the fact that we have a treasure that lies deep within us; nevertheless, for the devil to steal this treasure from us, he must break the clay jar. Did you know that for this reason, the devil, from the moment you were born, has been trying to break you? This insistent foe has not let one day go by without trying to destroy your faith, disrupt your peace, and steal your tranquility. From the day you were born, this antagonistic insomniac has not slept a wink trying to decode your hardware to determine what will make you break. With insatiable persistence, he is always scheming strategies to strip you of that treasure. Unfortunately, millions of people are oblivious to the unique treasure God placed in them before they were born. We've allowed other's opinions to take precedence over God's unique design for our lives. No longer can we allow the reflection of a mirror to dictate our condition. The Word of God states that we are made triune – spirit, soul and body (1 Thes 5:23). Considering this revelation, we come to the jaw-dropping conclusion that the all mighty mirror (our cultural god) has really only been reflecting 33.3% of who we really are. Perhaps this is the reason that the writer of Hebrews tells us that the soul and spirit can only be reflected and dissected by God's Word. The mirror will never reflect the treasure God placed in you. It will reflect the most insignificant part of us...our ever-aging body. For this reason, Paul states that, though we are aging and wasting away, our inner man (spirit) is being renewed daily. According to Paul, there is a God ordained perpetual rejuvenating effect occurring in us that can not be quantified.

Job did not go through the fire coincidently. He was a man of integrity. Did you know there's a price to pay for being honest, upright, and living a consecrated life to honor God? There will come moments when you will ask yourself: "Is serving God worth the sacrifice?" Is it worth it to endure the pain, the process of being fashioned into His likeness like the clay in the potter's hand?" But in the depths of your spirit, there will be a resounding affirmation, "Yes, it is worth it!" Nothing can be compared to the price that Christ paid for us on the cross of Calvary, carrying our sinful curse and diseases along with its death sentence. He took up what was rightfully ours so that we would have no penalty left to pay. Once crucified for our sake, He finally declared with a loud voice: "It is finished!" In the same way that Jesus fought and battled, we also should do the same until we hear: "Well done, good and faithful servant; you were faithful over a few things, I will make you ruler over many things. Enter into the joy of your lord" (Matthew 25:21). Paul is going through a transition in his spiritual life. God has plans, purposes and assignments prepared for him. Satan recognizes that he cannot allow Paul to continue to live because he will cause much damage to his demonic kingdom. We are reminded in Acts 19:15 that Paul has become popular in hell as the demon spirits confess that they know Paul. I can imagine a portrait of Paul highlighting one of the walls in hell, where there are pictures of "Hell's Most Wanted." While Paul's name reverberates throughout hell's corridors, the demons collectively seek him out to destroy him.

I do not want to be dogmatic, but I believe that sometimes the absence of attacks is indicative of the fact that we are not doing enough to be a threat to the kingdom of darkness. Why would the devil waste his demonic forces on someone who is not a menace to satan's empire? He has his gaze on those who, like you, are causing a revolution and reclaiming lost ground from the kingdom of darkness. Being exempt from satanic attacks does not necessarily mean that we are spiritually well.

In basketball, each team that plays and competes is composed of five players. At times a coach may direct two of his players to guard the other team's best player. Why? Because he represents a threat to the opposing team and can potentially cause defeat. Satan uses similar tactics with the most dangerous of believers. At times, he'll use a single demon, at other times he'll use legions. His tactics and schemes are endless. For that reason, when we are a spiritual threat, Satan does everything he can to extinguish our lives. But because we are protected and preserved for our assignment, 'No weapon formed against us will prosper.' It doesn't matter how many legions the devil sends to stop you from attaining the victory; with Christ, we outpower them.

As a spiritual being, Satan knew that he had to use the most potent weapons in his arsenal to destroy Paul and his ministry of discipling a generation and writing two-thirds of the New Testament. To kill him, he sent a viper. Not just an ordinary one, but a dangerous and venomous one. The adversary always uses his most potent weapons to steal, kill and destroy. He used Delilah to put a hit on Samson. Promiscuous Samson used to sleep around with prostitutes and with many other women, but Delilah was more than a one-night fling. She was more than a sexual encounter; she was on assignment. She was sent by the prince of the Philistines to expose the secret of Samson's great strength (Judges 16:5). Even though Delilah from afar looks like an ordinary prostitute looking for a hook-up, she was much more dangerous. Delilah was not sent to distract Samson, nor to make him sin, nor to entertain him, but rather to kill him. As you read this book, the devil is planning your demise. He prowls around like a roaring lion looking to devour you. When Paul discovers the viper, he notices that it is not like other vipers. Even though it appeared to be like the others, this one was different because it carried a deadly venom. Many attacks seem to be the same, but they are different. Like this particular venomous snake, some attacks carry a lethal dose of venom. Once induced, your life will take a critical turn for the worse and unless there's divine intervention, you will never be the same again. Some lesser attacks are sent to distract, discourage, diminish focus, damage (wound), but the attack on Paul has the specific intent to assassinate him. Jesus said it in John

10:10: "The thief does not come except to steal, and to kill, and to destroy." 1. *Steal,* violate, and deceive. 2. *Kill.* Death which means separation. Satan wants to separate you from your faith, from your hope and your love; he wants to cause you spiritual, emotional, and even physical death. 3. *Destroy.* To cease to exist; to tear down every pillar of faith, to snuff out every breath. That viper wanted to kill Paul and destroy the very person who would lay the foundation for the early church. As the key person that God would use to develop other leaders, Paul is on the devil's hit list. The attack, then, is an indicator of a purposeful, powerful call by God!

In the previous chapter, I felt tempted to finish this book when the viper died in the fire. It seemed to me that the biblical story had provided you with a good introduction and developed into a contentious plot followed by a climactic ending which was brought upon by the death of the serpent. However, I had to continue writing and you'll have to keep on reading because the serpent was poisonous. Because we are now dealing with a venomous attack, the death of the serpent means absolutely nothing. You see, the danger doesn't lie in the serpent, it lies in the deadly dose of lethal venom that is running through Paul's body. The moment this viper sinks its fangs into Paul's hand, it injects a fatal dose of venom, enough to end his life. The people around him simply watch in horror and wait for the inevitable to occur. The venom's reputation precedes it and can be summarized in one word...Undefeated. Throughout its life, this viper had caused monumental wreckage. It had shortened the lives of many. It is famous for dashing the dreams of multitudes. Paul is a heavy underdog who will surely become its next victim. Though Paul can feel the anguish, no one sees the venom running through Paul's bloodstream. His cardiovascular system has turned into portals of lava, running through his whole body. The venom's tormenting pain makes death almost appealing to Paul.

The venom has four functions to carry out in the body of its victim:

**Pain.** The *first* effect is to produce pain. It has been proven that a viper that weighs five pounds can kill a lion that weighs three hundred pounds. Pain spreads throughout the body until it contaminates the entire blood supply. Every second that goes by is deadly. The pain takes over every limb with the ability to cause permanent damage. Even the mind falls victim to this terrible pain. Thoughts are sabotaged, and the mind is taken captive. Reasoning becomes distorted, ideas are confused, and one's strength is weakened. Just as the viper's venom can conquer the king of the jungle; in the same way, a human being can also be controlled by this unbearable pain. Perhaps you're familiar with the effects of venomous pain because you were victimized years ago. When you were born, the enemy designed a deadly potion with your name on it. You may have forgotten the time when the viper first attacked you, but when you least expect it, a memory will come in the form of a flashback. Unbeknownst to us, we go through life dealing with that "pain," which after a while seems normal because our bodies have the amazing ability to adapt to whatever is abnormal or discomforting. We try to deaden the pain or cover it up temporarily by adopting bad habits or an unhealthy lifestyle. There are men who were ignored by their father during their childhood and were never able to develop a healthy relationship. As adults, they try to conceal the void by toughening up, yet still carry the painful memories of that venomous attack. You see, if not dealt with, this venom will affect not only you but everyone you love. Your spouse, children, grandchildren and generations to come will suffer from the effects of a generational attack. Not able to control their actions, they imitate the same behavior of the person who caused them pain, and they continue to repeat it and pass it on to others. Wounded people wound others. Pain makes no exception. It attacks and controls whoever has been exposed to its deadly venom. It does not matter what your social level or economic status is—rich, middle class, or impoverished—pain has a deadly effect that causes emotional ruin in everyone. First it wears you down; then it depletes your strength and your courage, until it finally destroys your hopes and dreams.

Perhaps at this very moment you're thinking of giving up on something God has inspired you to do. Maybe you're perplexed and your dreams, desires, and vision for tomorrow only seem like a fantasy. The only thing that stands out clearly in your mind are the failures of the past. It could very well be that the venom induced in you years ago is still affecting you, in hopes that you would abandon all that you were born to accomplish. He knows you have abilities, gifts, and talents that God has given you, and that you are a serious threat to him here on earth.

Pain has its benefits. It functions as an alarm to warn the body that something is wrong. The worst thing you can do is ignore the warnings. Doctors say that most heart attacks can be avoided because there almost always are symptoms that the victim ignores. Many, knowing that they are in danger, refuse to go to the hospital for fear of a negative medical diagnosis. When they finally decide to go, the damage has already been done. As you read this book, I would like for you to examine your life. If you are ignoring a particular area in your life and have pain that no one is aware of, I want you to address it and give it to the Lord right now. Perhaps you are battling with disillusionment. You thought at this juncture in life you'd be way ahead of the game and it's caused you to contemplate quitting altogether. Seek God earnestly, ask the Holy Spirit to highlight what areas you must surrender or turn over to Him so that the power of God can flow in a supernatural way. Perhaps you're asking why? And the answer is: Because no matter our age, color or creed, every human being, regardless of religious affiliation has been made in the image of God. As his "best" creation, we (humanity) were made the most beautiful and perfect creation.

Our quality of life changes for the better the moment we surrender our lives to the Lord. God's will for you is to experience the *zoé* life; that is, the life of God manifested in us. Turn over to the Lord all your worries and pains. He cares for you (1 Peter 5:7). At times, the pain is introduced through betrayal by a family member, a friend, or a brother in the faith. Whatever the reason, the result is always the same: unbearable pain. During our preaching revivals, we were puzzled when we saw that more than 70 percent of active believers in the faith came forward to have God get rid of their pain. Sometimes, the pain was from long ago, and it was tolerated and accepted as a part of life. This is exactly what Satan wants: for us to make a bed for the pain so that it becomes a part of our daily walk. Once you have become desensitized to pain, it will lose its function, no longer alerting us to impending danger. I believe God has allowed me to write this book to help provide deliverance to people who are seeking complete freedom. If you are experiencing greater faith and extraordinary encouragement, it is the Holy Spirit who is actively near you to transform your life right now. If you want to become truly free from this terrible torment, say the following prayer out loud:

Holy Father, I surrender my life to you. I turn this area _____ (be specific) over to you, which has caused me great pain. I close the specific door that was opened by me or someone else. I take responsibility and seal it shut and apply the blood of Jesus over it. In the name of Jesus and with the authority of God and His Word, I renounce every hurtful feeling that has controlled my life and my destiny. I break allegiance with pain, and I declare that Jesus Christ is my Lord and Savior...Amen.

*Paralysis*. As if the pain weren't enough, there is another effect from the venom—paralysis. Paralysis is, in part, a result of pain, but it occurs when the neurological system is damaged. The electrical signals from the brain are sent to the dorsal spine (the center of the nervous system), but a break occurs in the circuit. The neurological system has been damaged. Webster's Dictionary defines paralysis as "a loss or impediment of voluntary movement." The Oxford Dictionary defines it as "the lack of ability to move normally." Imagine not being able to move yourself in the capacity or with the potential you were created. Not being able to use your physical abilities brings with it great frustration. The word frustration means "preventing a person from reaching their goal or making them feel useless." Can you identify with that? The devil wants to sidetrack you from your way so that you don't reach the land that flows with milk and honey. This deadly venom is guaranteed to kill and destroy you. Paul is in line to be the poisonous snake's next victim. I'm sure Paul could have been just another victim on this serpent's list. Perhaps you can identify with this chapter and feel a certain connection because you recognize the areas in your life where you are suffering paralysis. Can you recall the good times when you had movement in your extremities? You could stand up on your feet, walk, and move around with ease without having to depend on anyone. As you remember the freedom you once enjoyed, you delight in the memory, but at the same time experience bittersweet feelings. When you ponder on your lack of movement, you feel frustration, despair, and even contempt. Before the attack came, you used to enjoy a constant and enjoyable communion with God. Being able to talk with Almighty God was not seen as a task, but rather a privilege. The ability to love was so normal that you didn't have to force yourself, but rather love flowed daily in a supernatural way. You loved the people you knew as well as those you didn't know. Reading the Bible was a great delight. The Bible wasn't a foreign book, but a map and guide that served as a lamp to your feet and a light to your path. Each word filled your heart with plenty of wisdom and faith. Words such as unattainable, improbable or impossible—had no place in your vocabulary. Do you remember the confidence and joy you had, along with the desire to live an abundant life? The desire to please God in everything had no limits. From the moment you opened your eyes until you closed them to sleep, you walked in integrity because of your consciousness to the Word of God. Despite the surrounding issues that continuously threaten us, be they political, generational, global, both nationally and economically, you lived in a present peace that few experience, a profound peace that those around you could not comprehend.

But now, the venom has caused paralysis in your life. The fact that you attend church, are part of a volunteer group, started a business or have attained a high level of education has not been sufficient to deliver you from your chronic condition. Like many victims who suffer from paralysis, when they recognize their present situation, then remember the past, they are filled with dissatisfaction and depression. Their focus changes from fighting against the enemy to fighting against themselves. They fight against self-rejection when they consider their spiritual or emotional condition, and instead of feeling contentment, they feel hate and resentment toward themselves. They blame others for their sad state, and they ignore the one who is the real culprit, Satan, the author of their trauma, the one who causes death and destruction, the one who brings spiritual calamity and paralysis to their lives. "We know that we are of God, and the whole world lies under the control of the wicked one" (1 John 5:19).

Knowing what we must do and not being able to do anything brings frustration. When Paul began his ministry, he said the following: "For the good that I will to do, I do not do; but the evil I will not to do, that I practice" (Romans 7:19). Perhaps you are a person who would like to be a model student, an exemplary father, a loving husband, a providing mother, but paralysis prevents you from doing it. Perhaps you are a woman of destiny and of promising purpose. Your desire is to fulfill the expectations other people have put on you. You want to be the virtuous woman of Proverbs 31: a mother who takes care of her household, who leads her children by wise example and is a wife who can encourage and complement her husband, so he can fulfill the purposes of God for which he was called. Do you desire to raise, nurture, and feed your family with the abilities, gifts, and talents God has put in you, but because of the paralysis, you have not been able to achieve it? Perhaps you are a young person with a brilliant life ahead of you. You have all the resources and abilities to carve out for yourself an outstanding future. You want to make a significant investment in your generation, and perhaps you feel you are the last hope for someone in your family to excel. The pressures are immense, no one understands your pain and frustration, meanwhile, there are plenty of people trying to diagnose your paralysis. There is no lack of advice from people with good intentions. However, everything continues along without change. The torment has caused a lot of internal doubts in your life. Confusion and insecurity have been the norm in the depths of your soul. The loneliness, sadness, and lack of confidence have ruled your present life. All of this has been at a great cost. Your spiritual strength has been diminished. The Bible speaks about our youth: "Strength is your glory," but you still are weak to the point of immobility due to the paralysis from which you're suffering. I know colleagues who are going through this horrible phase called "paralysis." Many of them pastors, evangelists, teachers, prophets, and apostles who are dealing with frustrations that stem from ministerial paralysis. I also know high-level professionals who are paralyzed, and irregardless of the accolades they collect, they can't seem to break their cycle of defeat. God has called you, even from childhood, to a specific purpose. You have seen God's hand at work. You have experienced the magnitude and faithfulness of the Lord. You have had moments of success and indescribable visitations from the Spirit of God, but the venomous snake has sunk its fangs into you and injected that deadly venom into the heart of your ministry or business. Since then, you have not been able to function as God intended you to, from before the time He created and called you. It seems as if your strength has disappeared, you don't trust any-one, and you become more discouraged by the minute. The vision that God once placed in you has become a vague memory. You preach by profession, not by con-viction. Prayer has become a traditional ritual. Perhaps your marriage is suffering from the consequences of your paralysis. You realize your family members are also victims of the same syndrome. This paralysis that has come upon them has taken an even bigger toll because they depend on you to free them. Whether you're a pastor or a blue/white collar worker, know that your freedom is a prayer away. If you believe with your heart and confess with your mouth that Jesus is your savior, I believe that your breakthrough will come to pass.

If freedom is not acquired it will be impossible to give what you do not have. While Peter and John were going to the synagogue to pray, they encountered an ungodly man who was lame and poor. Fixing his eyes on him, Peter said to him: "Silver and gold I do not have, but what I do have I give you" (Acts 3:6). And this man, lame from birth, was healed, because he benefited from what Peter and John had...the healing power of the Holy Spirit. Friend, if we are paralyzed, we will never be able to give what we do not have. When you board a plane, flight attendants caution all passengers that if the plane loses cabin pressure, oxygen masks will descend from the above panel, and they warn us to make sure we first place the mask on ourselves before placing one on the person traveling with us. I believe the most painful thing is knowing that we are not giving to others what we should be giving them, simply because we are paralyzed. The most dangerous effect of paralysis is that it doesn't allow the body to feel pain. It almost comforts the body in order to execute a paralytic state.

Pain serves as a warning from the body, letting you know something is wrong. Pain also serves to let you know there's danger or something is abnormal. When the nerves are damaged, the body is at risk. The lack of feeling can cause serious problems. I have heard of people who suffered severe burns on their bodies just because they couldn't feel heat. One of the serious effects of spiritual paralysis is that at times it hinders us from hearing (sensing) the voice of the Holy Spirit. We can be in the presence of God and not feel Him. Nor can we feel His conviction or His warning whenever we are close to danger. David cried out to God when he stopped feeling the joy of his salvation because he was paralyzed by his sin. It is necessary that we know God's attributes. Scripture assures us that God will not despise a contrite and humble heart. When paralysis takes control of the soul, it cripples your vision and your hopes for the future. Once gripped by this awful stage of venom, prayer becomes laborious because we feel distant from God; our prayers seem to hit what appears to be brass heavens and walls of iron. We constantly battle with insensibility and numbness... although our relationship with God is not based on feelings; but compassion is a needed sentiment in order to see God respond to a need.

We know that times of testing will come, and we must persevere until we receive an answer. That is something expected and standard in the normal life of a believer. But when all feeling is lost for months or years because of a trauma, we must understand that this is not God's normal plan. Examine yourself right now. Are you battling with indifference? Do you know that you must forgive, but you don't feel like doing it? Should you love, but you don't feel like doing it? Should you trust, but you don't feel like doing it? Should you ask for forgiveness, but you don't feel like doing it? The

Word of God teaches us how we should live, think, and act. Having difficulty in obeying scripture or submitting to authority should be sufficient reason to concern us. Paralysis is frustrating. It is used by the enemy of our souls to make us feel useless regarding the calling, service, and purpose God has predestined for us.

**Swelling.** As if the pain and the paralysis weren't enough, the third stage is swelling. The dictionary defines the word swelling as an "enlargement caused by internal pressure." When Paul was attacked by the viper, everyone was waiting for him to swell up. The physical evidence that the victim was going to die was swelling. Swelling is caused by the accumulation of water and toxins that the body retains when the natural filters no longer function. Kidneys are the body's filter. They purify the blood and cleanse the water. The blood depends on these organs to maintain its function and provide life. The venom from vipers cause swelling because the kidneys shut down, disallowing the blood to filter, and causing the body to become poisoned, which eventually ends up causing death. Ephesians 5:26 teaches us that the Word of God will "cleanse [us] with the washing of water by the word." The enemy will desperately try to put you in a situation where your "kidneys" cannot function. The "kidneys" of the believer is the Word of God. The Word is the filter for our spirit, soul, and body. Is it a coincidence that the first thing we stop doing when we're attacked is reading the Word of God? We can read newspapers, magazines, books, and even spend a multiplicity of hours in front of the television. But when it comes to the Bible, we are suddenly overcome with irresistible tiredness and weariness. We not only stop reading the Bible, but we also stop meditating on it, believing it, confessing it, sharing it and applying it. When we stop reading, believing, and confessing the Word of God, it becomes impossible to apply it to our lives. The devil knows what Psalm 1 says: "And in His law (the Word of God) he meditates day and night. He shall be like a tree planted by the rivers of water, that brings forth its fruit in its season, whose leaf also shall not wither" (vv. 2–3).

Satan is the one who causes spiritual droughts in your life. He dries up portals that are designated to give us life: our hearts, marriages, relationships. The benefits of knowing the Word of God are plentiful. When you guard the Word of God in your heart, and obey it, then Joshua 1:8 will come to pass: "For then you will make your way prosperous, and then you will have good success." With this truth in mind, it is essential that our spiritual "kidneys" continue to function normally. The venom causes the kidneys to stop functioning, and the Word of God stops having an effect in your life. Before the attack came to traumatize you, the Word of God was the anchor of your soul. It served as a compass, or GPS. So many have discovered the importance of having a relationship with God's Word. It is not just another Bible app or historical book but God's instruction manual that gives us a glimpse of the mind of our creator: what pleases him, what expectations he has of us and our entire benefits package. Nevertheless, when you study the birth and development of the early church, you will notice that during that historical time a countless number of believers dedicated their lives to copying the original biblical manuscripts, allowing them to be passed from one generation to the next. These men sacrificed their lives and spilt their blood to preserve the Word of God. The danger is in not reading and believing the Word of God. Why? Because this Word is the foundation of our faith (Romans 10:17). It is the anchor of our promises. Our prayers, intercessions, pleas, and supplications are backed up by this sacred manual of instructions called the Word of God. Within its pages, we discover our inheritance and instructions to obey our Lord. His complete plan and will for our lives are in the Bible.

Without discounting the dreams and supernatural visions, the Holy Scriptures are the primary way that God communicates with His people. I am convinced that many Christians today die spiritually because they do not have a strong biblical foundation. Many are suffering the effects of a life disconnected from God's counsel and therefore are making impulsive decisions. If statistics are true - the divorce rate at 52% in America, 80% of college graduates never working in the field related to their bachelor's degree, and less than 3% of Christian university graduates going into full-time ministry - then I question where we are getting our counsel and guidance from. Jesus said: "If you abide in Me, and My words abide in you, you will ask what you desire, and it shall be done for you" (John 15:7). His Word in us is what makes the difference! The common denominator to receive what we ask for is conditional: "If His Word remains in us, let us ask whatever we want," (not what we need). How will God give us everything that we want? The secret is when we abide in Him and His Word abides in us, we are going to ask Him in accordance with His perfect will. We know His will because His Word is in us. The will of God is in His Word. If we read and apply it, we will not have to worry about asking for something outside of His will or asking for something against His will.

Once the Word of God is no longer being read as a result of the venom, our lives begin to swell up. They swell up because the internal pressures have disfigured and contaminated us. At times, the attacks and traumas disfigure us, and we no longer look like the person God created. Once we swell up and portray the disfiguration that comes with this condition, we stop representing the image and likeness of God Almighty. Just as our body fills up with toxins, our emotional life also becomes contaminated with other types of toxins: doubt, fear, anxiety, hate, rancor, resentment, low self-esteem, depression, and others. The Oxford Dictionary tells us that toxins are caused by venom. If these toxins remain in your system without the Word of God functioning as a purifier and filter, your spiritual life will eventually end and every dream you have in your spiritual bosom will be aborted. The Word of God is also our mirror (James 1:23–24). Besides studying it, I like to use it to examine and see my reflection, like a mirror. If what is reflected in the mirror is not what God designed for me, I know I'm in grave danger and need divine instruction and His immediate help. At this point I would like you to pause and look at your life. What is your reflection like? Are you pleased with what you see in the mirror, or do you notice that it isn't what the Lord planned for you? My prayer is that the Holy Spirit shows you the will of the Father and the divine plan that He ordained for you.

**Asphyxiation.** The last phase of the attack is asphyxiation. That is the cause of death. The asphyxiation is caused by suffocation. Suffocation occurs when you're not inhaling sufficient oxygen. This happens when the venom causes swelling, which hinders the oxygen from flowing through the respiratory tract. The trachea is the track that oxygen uses to enter through the mouth or nose to get to the lungs. With swelling, this track closes due to pressure, and the person lapses into a state of unconsciousness before dying. Fighting for breath is a desperate and agonizing moment. Something that was so natural to do, such as breathing, now turns into a fight for life. The track we use to breathe and keep ourselves alive is our relationship with God. Our relationship with God is what keeps us alive and joyful in Christ. The anchor of our soul is being able to wake up each morning with life to pray and praise our God. When someone enters this last stage of not being able to communicate or breathe as they had before, it is cause for desperation and for becoming anxious and fearful. We did not realize until now how natural it was to inhale and exhale. Medical science describes these actions of inhaling and exhaling as involuntary movements. This means that, without thinking about it beforehand, we inhale and exhale involuntarily; they are automatic actions or reflexes. In the same manner, when we are living according to His perfect will, it is natural to breathe the breath of God. The stage of asphyxiation is divided into three phases: the fight to breathe, unconsciousness, and death.

The fight to breathe. The fight with the respiratory tract occurs due to a tracheal blockage. What is blocking your life that hinders you from having communion with God? What is hindering the closeness you once had and now long for? Now you find yourself in the stage where you feel that with each second that passes, you're losing strength, courage, and hope. You see others around you laughing and breathing with great ease. You ask yourself, "What's wrong with me?", finding yourself in a stage even more desperate: You're unconscious.

Unconsciousness. When you enter the stage of unconsciousness, you stop fighting. Your strength and courage have left you. You feel totally helpless. You are focusing on the words the devil has whispered in your ears that say: "You have lost everything: your spiritual inheritance, your marriage, your youth, your integrity, your ministry, your dreams, and your destiny." And even though you're not interested in listening to the opinion of the enemy, you have no other choice because you are spiritually and emotionally unconscious.

Death. Finally, death comes—separation—which is the last stage. Not able to receive oxygen, your heart stops beating. Death is the stage when the spirit separates from the physical body. When you die spiritually, the devil assumes final control because you are separated from God and are at the mercy of your body. All the decisions and plans for your earthly life are now directed by the carnal man. It is sad to see someone make impulsive and rash decisions.

I have known a good number of believers who were once on fire and obedient to God's plan. However, they allowed the enemy to disconnect them from the "respiratory tract," which is the presence of Jehovah. Death is one of the saddest occurrences for anyone. Death was never in God's plans for humanity but came as a byproduct of disobedience. Knowing that the person you care for has transitioned to another place, where they will be separated from you, is reason for sadness. Even though, from a human perspective, we know that a follower of Christ has a better destiny after death, it still brings tears and pain. But what will happen to that person who does not have the hope of a better destiny? The Spirit of God, who dwells in us, cries and sympathizes with those who allow the enemy to determine their spiritual death. Jesus said that Satan came to steal, kill, and destroy (John 10:10). This spiritual death separates you totally from God. The sad thing about it is that at times we believe that because we belong to a church or a council, we are exempt from spiritual death. There are so many people just existing and waiting to be buried because they died a long time ago. They've lost all hope and are just going through the motions. Even those who have the assignment to dispense hope to the lost soul through the art of preaching, are preaching from catacombs because they are nothing more than living cadavers. They do not have a fresh word or an anointing that follows them because their relationship with God is dead. The reason many leave church in the same condition as when they arrived is because they are numb. The gathering resembles more a mausoleum than a place where the Holy Spirit ministers to those in attendance.

Many are experiencing emotional death, which is equally dangerous. Your emotions consist of your mind, will, and desires. When you die emotionally, it is impossible to fulfill God's plan for your life. There are women who suffer from an inferiority complex because of their husbands, and they have not been able to recover their emotional health. Spiritually they are fine, they are active in the church, and they persevere, but their emotions have not been healed. Daily they remember and relive traumas that cause them pain in their private life. The devil lies to them, saying they must act like clowns, smiling on the outside, but crying on the inside. Some become experts in concealing their pain so that they can perform their tasks and responsibilities. Emotional death is sad because we cannot apply the Word of God to our lives nor receive the blessings God has for us. An example of this is what the Bible refers to in Ephesians 1:3: "Blessed be the God and Father of our Lord Jesus

Christ, who has blessed us with every spiritual blessing in the heavenly places in Christ." It is impossible to receive and apply this continual blessing if we do not allow it to be conveyed to our mind. Ephesians 4:23 says: "...and be renewed in the spirit of your mind." Since we are more than conquerors through the One who loved us, we must allow our spirit access to our emotions, no matter what situations seem to threaten us. God has given us His powerful Word so that it is available to us, but we must meditate on it day and night (Joshua 1:8) so that everything goes well for us and we truly prosper. Our mind plays an important role in obtaining and maintaining the victory. We must bring to pass the victories that belong to us according to the Word of God. Dr. Tim Warner says:

1. Your mind tells you: "You are a sinner because you sin." The Word says: "You are a saint (whom God has declared righteous) who sins." 2. Your mind tells you: "You are what you do." The Word says: "You were made in the image and likeness of God." 3. Your mind tells you: "Your identity comes from what people say about you." The Word says: "Your identity comes from what the Lord says about you." 4. Your mind tells you: "Your conduct tells you what you should believe about yourself." The Word says: "Your belief about yourself determines your conduct."

"For as he thinks in his heart, so is he" (Proverbs 23:7). The key word is think. If you let your thoughts run with the wind, you will never have thoughts shaped and molded by God's Word. It is crucial that our identity be healthy and anchored in the Word of God. The believer who has his thoughts filtered by the Word of God possesses a healthy and correct perspective and perception before God.

# DISCUSSION QUESTIONS FOR CHAPTER 5

1. Can you relate to the four phases of poisoning? If so, how?
   - Pain
   - Paralysis
   - Swelling
   - Asphyxiation

2. Write down four things you could do to counter these phases:

3. In what ways can you experience the "zoé" life?

# CHAPTER 6

# THEY'RE PLANNING YOUR FUNERAL

However, they were expecting that he would swell up or suddenly fall dead. (Acts 28:6) God created us for a great purpose. The destroyer of souls intends to fight tirelessly to destroy the destiny designed by God for your life. However, this God ordained destiny is conditional. God told Moses: "You shall enter the Promised Land." But because he did not obey God, it was Joshua who entered. God also promised David: "You will build me a temple," but because he did not obey God, it was his son Solomon who built it. Paul said to Timothy, "This charge I commit to you son, Timothy, according to the prophecies previously made concerning you, that by them you may wage the good warfare" (1 Timothy 1:18). We must fight so that God's promises are fulfilled in our lives as He wishes. God assures Moses that He will be with him and will use him to free the people of Israel from the Egyptians. He explains to him what signs and wonders He will perform to confirm His Word so that Pharaoh sees that Moses has Jehovah's backing. But suddenly, God gets angry with Moses and looks for him to kill him. What happened between verses 23 and 24 in the fourth chapter of Exodus? God delights in Moses, and first He commissions him to carry orders to confront Pharaoh; then, he looks for Moses to kill him. His wife Zipporah takes a sharp flint stone, circumcises his son and throws the baby's foreskin at Moses' feet. This intervention by Zipporah appeases God, who then has mercy on Moses. Moses seemed to think that because he had an intimate relationship with Jehovah, he did not have to circumcise his son on the eighth day, according to Jewish law. Nevertheless, he was under a wrong impression, just as many ministers are today. They believe that their many years in the ministry exempt them from obeying God's law. At times, we believe that the more titles we gain or the more years we have in ministry, the more entitled we are, deceiving many to take shortcuts or detours. We err when we do not obey the laws or commandments given by God. Notice, that although God had called Moses and promised to use him to free His people, now he seeks to kill him. Don't take God's call or His promises lightly ; let us be obedient to please God in everything. Delayed obedience is disobedience! You control your own destiny.

When Paul is attacked by the viper, everyone expected him to fall over dead. The enemy of our souls waits for you to fail. He wants to get rid of you as soon as possible. Considering all that has happened in your life, the devil is planning your funeral. Considering the multiplicity of victims who have succumbed to the attack and died, I can imagine Paul being surrounded by doubt and pessimism. I'm sure some must have thought, "time to dig another grave." All of them were expecting him to die. It is possible that some wanted him to suffer a slow death, because they believed it was God's judgment on him. Others, perhaps, were rejoicing for what awaited him. And there were those who didn't care that he was facing death. During the chaos that developed as a result of the incident, a crowd began to form to see what would happen next. All of them were waiting for Paul to die. It is very probable that they began to calculate how many breaths he had left before expiring. They waited and waited and continued to wait.

It is incredible how this event can seem to resemble the attacks against our own lives. The devil and his army place a great deal of emphasis on usurping any hope you may have that can lead to your miracle or healing. Once Satan has you on the ropes, he relentlessly tries to finish you off. This is the time where the Apostle James reminds us to submit ourselves to God, resist the devil and he will flee. In Greek, the word flee means to run in terror. If you want to hurt the devil, submit your entire game plan to the Lord and resist his attacks instead of caving under pressure. This is why conditioning your spirit, soul and body to worship God in the midst of the storm is so devastating to the kingdom of darkness...If you find yourself under attack, place the bookmark on this page and go take a praise break...Go ahead and march around your house and glorify God in the midst of the pain...How was that? Amazing, I bet! True praise and worship is spontaneous. Don't wait for your church to conduct a service to be lead into a time of praise and worship. Learn how to be an unpredictable praiser and worshipper. *"I shall bless the Lord at all times his praises shall continuously be in my mouth."* (Psalm 34:1 NLT)

Instead of taking an antidepressant when you feel those symptoms that want to control your mind and your body, look for the Bible and begin to sing psalms to the Lord. Do not give Satan the satisfaction by reacting with fear and insecurity. Before you picked up this book, God already had your deliverance. I want you to know that during these difficult and incomprehensible times, God is on your side and with the faithfulness of a true friend, He wants to help you. While you're going through trial by fire, the demons are celebrating.

While you're reading this book, your enemies are preparing your funeral. They are rehearsing the eulogy they will recite in front of your grave. Others will shine your coffin, smiling and cheering their heads off: "Finally, _____ (your name) has died! He'll no longer cause us havoc and great loss. We'll no longer have to reinforce our gates because of him." Our enemies are not just spiritual; they are also carnal enemies (Psalm 3). They are purchasing their black suits, so they can parade at your funeral. They are preparing your headstone; they're rehearsing their condolences.

Look around you carefully. All of them are present at your funeral. The devil and his demons, your enemies, are all celebrating. The headstone has your name and your birth date inscribed, along with the predicted date of your spiritual death. The enemy put it there. They have dug the hole, and those who have witnessed the last scene of your life are anxious for the funeral home director to begin the funeral service. Everyone is ready. Preparations have been made, and the enemy is happy; but there's a problem...

The coffin is empty. Ask yourself this question: Did I subscribe to die prematurely? God has provided you with everything necessary for you to live according to John 10:10. There is nothing worse than feeling the pain of rejection. When you see everyone celebrating your death, you feel the cruelty of such an act. Christ can sympathize and identify with your pain. During His last twelve hours, from the moment He was arrested in the garden of Gethsemane, Jesus suffered at the hands of mockers and torturers. The Jews, whom He came to seek and save, were the first to condemn him to death. Where were the multitudes he had fed? Where were the droves of those he had healed? Where is Bartemeus, the delivered man at Gadara, the woman who had an issue of blood, or the Samaritan woman? Surely, they had heard about the crucifixion of the Christ. Other than John, where were the disciples? If there is anyone who can sympathize with our weaknesses, it's Christ, the Savior of the world. Whenever you feel abandoned and/or rejected, remember Jesus can relate to your feelings of abandonment. His Word says that He was tempted in everything. I'm sure that Jesus was tempted to not want to die when he prayed to the Father, saying: "O My Father, if it is possible, let this cup pass from Me; nevertheless, not as I will but as You will" (Matthew 26:39). Jesus is asking the Father to free him from the torment.

The most precious gift God gives to human beings is free will. Self-will; the freedom to choose for ourselves. It is a powerful weapon that God has given to humanity. The heart of God is filled with happiness when, by our own will, we surrender to Him so that He can do with us whatever He wills. "He gave His only begotten Son, that whoever believes in Him should not perish but have everlasting life" (John 3:16). Now it is our turn to accept or reject His will. We have the power to make the decision to continue as good soldiers of the faith or give up on the journey. Jesus said: "The kingdom of heaven suffers violence, and the violent take it by force" (Matthew 11:12). Notice that this applies to those who have determined not to lose but to win; those who are going to receive their reward from God. I want to tell you that your victory lies in your determination not to lose. The woman who suffered from a flow of blood opted not to die. By her persistent faith she obtained her healing, and although she practically had to crawl, she made a way through the crowd that surrounded her. Without doubt, in her intent to reach Jesus, she was criticized, kicked, had dirt thrown in her face, and suffered humiliation. Nevertheless, she held on to her decision firmly. And through her fervor and perseverance, she succeeded in obtaining her miracle. She was rewarded with virtue and healing from the Lord. Blind Bartimaeus received his sight, but he had to cry out until the Lord heard him. Christ voluntarily stripped Himself of His glory, His omnipresence, His omniscience and His omnipotence. Like a lamb, He was carried to the slaughterhouse. When Peter cut off Malchus' right ear, the servant to the high priest, Jesus rebuked him, saying: "Do you think I cannot now pray to My Father, and he will provide Me with more than twelve legions of angels?" (Matthew 26:53). In this instance, Jesus reveals the essence of His voluntary humility and how He keeps Himself in the perfect will of the Father. In His omniscience, the Father has seen your pain. He knows the horrific events you have suffered, but despite all of that, the enemy still cannot invade or manipulate your will. You must make the decision to continue until you reach the next level with God. Friend, look at what has happened to you. Consider the course of your life; it has been painful, but with purposes ordained by God. You cannot give up now. If you believe, you will see God's purpose manifested at its designated time. Hang in there! If you feel like you are hanging by a thread, make sure it's the hem of his garment. If you keep fighting to resist the evil one, I assure you that at the right time God will make it His responsibility to honor you.

Several years ago, I spoke to a cardiologist, and he explained to me that a young person has less chance of surviving a heart attack than an older person. That's because as a person grows older, their heart builds new veins. Those veins are called subsidiary veins. The phrase "subsidiary guarantee" is very popular among financial institutions that measure the value of possessions that their clients have accumulated over time.

While the heart beats millions of times over a long period, it builds new veins that are absolutely necessary. If an older person suffers a heart attack, the subsidiary veins absorb most of the impact, saving the person from greater damage. Even though the heart of a young person is much stronger than that of an older person, when they suffer a heart attack, it is fatal in most cases, because they lack those subsidiary veins. "And we know that all things work together for good" (Romans 8:28). With each circumstance that comes to your life, be it an attack, a trauma, a fight or a test, remember that whatever it is, you are building subsidiary veins. Without realizing it, you're developing a stronger anointing that will counter the attacks of the enemy in the name of Jesus Christ. Don't look to your enemies, because you will surely become discouraged. I am convinced that Paul said to himself: "You called me to suffer for your Name, to preach Your Word to the Gentiles, and to the kings and sons of Israel; your mission for my life still has not ended." Paul understands he has a special calling on his life, and the devil is in no way happy about it. In that crucial moment, Paul does not waste his time looking at those who were present: he looks to the future, the plan, purpose, and mission God has for his life. Considering the entirety of God's plan and the role he was to play in that plan, Paul was not ready to die. Examine your life now and think about what God has freed you from. Do you believe your life should end this way? There is a purpose and a plan that still have not totally come to pass. The present attack, just like the one that helped Paul fulfill his ministry, will help to shape you to be the kind of person God can use. Don't let this present attack destroy you. Use it as an experience and determine in your spirit to persevere until the end. Refuse to live, pray, and act according to what others say or try to pressure you to do. I prefer to live according to what God says and thinks about me and not what the present situation is dictating, for it will soon pass away.

## THE DECISION IS YOURS

Paul makes the decision to live and not to die—and to believe God. What decision will you choose? Even though you have experienced a shipwreck, storm, cold, rain, and a snake bite, God has remained by your side, ready to free you from every unexplainable situation. Many of us do not understand what is happening to us, but God sees it and understands everything. He is waiting for you to decide what you're going to do: either continue in His plan or abandon everything. God cannot operate nor manifest Himself in your life unless you decide not to die. Invite Him to show His power in your life. He promises not to despise a contrite and humble heart.

# DISCUSSION QUESTIONS FOR CHAPTER 6

1. What are some major attacks you are suffering right now?

2. Explain the term subsidiary veins. In what ways are they beneficial?

3. Describe three ways in which you have decided to live and not die.

4. In what way will you invite God to demonstrate His power in your life?

5. When you look at the future, what do you visualize regarding God's plan, purpose, and mission for your life?

# CHAPTER 7

# THE ANTIDOTE

*That good thing, which was committed to you, keep by the Holy Spirit who dwells in us.* (2 Timothy 1:14) What did Paul possess that did not allow him to die like any other victim? I often ask myself: What did the early church have that enabled them to refuse the temptation to deny their faith? They had resolve of spirit that made them willing to face every persecution, even unto death. The history of martyrs tells of entire families that were devoured by lions just for refusing to deny their faith. The stories of many who suffered and were tortured are still a well-known subject among many people—accounts of men and women who were willing to use their final moments on this earth for an eternal purpose. Jesus did the same in His final moments. I can picture the disciples, with tears in their eyes, as they listened attentively to His last words. They knew that the time had come for their master, hero, and spiritual father to be put to death. Luke writes in his Gospel (24:49) what Jesus said to His disciples: "Behold, I send the Promise of My Father upon you; but tarry in the city of Jerusalem until you are endued with power from on high." Perhaps they asked: "Power? What power, and why?" Luke also shares Christ's last words in Acts 1:8 - "But you shall receive power when the Holy Spirit has come upon you; and you shall be witnesses to Me in Jerusalem, and in all Judea and Samaria, and to the end of the earth." It is interesting that the word witnesses is *martus* in Greek, which translates to martyr. After studying this subject for quite some time, I understood that Jesus knew they would give their lives for Him. They would not proceed a single step without being filled with divine power...That divine power...The baptism of the Holy Spirit.

The power on the Day of Pentecost was paramount for the disciples to fulfill their divine assignment, which was to give up their lives so that the gospel could continue trailblazing a path for all to follow, though bloody, yet eternal. When we compare the primitive church to the modern church of today, we see there has been a falling away from the urgent responsibility of evangelizing, not only in the church but also amongst believers. Many people today cross our paths, become our neighbors, yet the majority will never even hear a peep from us concerning Jesus. We work or study with unbelievers yet we don't dare to speak to them about Christ. We are surrounded by people whom await an eternity of doom in hell, ignoring the subject completely, because of shame or it being a bother. Just thinking about moving out of our comfort zone causes us discomfort. As a pastor, I would say that if, once again, we will become a bold church, it will have to start with a love revolution. After all, the message of the gospel is one of compassion, love and boldness. We have defined the Holy Spirit as an object or a thing, but not as a person. Metaphorically, the Bible uses symbols (wind, dove, fire, water, oil, rivers of living water) to give a description of His attributes. However, we have done a poor job teaching about His personality. The Holy Spirit is the third Person of the Trinity, and He is God. God is not only with us or for us, but God is in us. Think about it this way: God is living in you!

Paul did not fall victim to the serpent because God was with him. When the bush was burning in the desert next to Mount Sinai, the miracle was not the fact that a voice was heard coming out of it, but rather that the bush was not consumed by the fire. The miracle is not that you're going through the fire, the phenomenon is that despite the hell you're going through, you're not consumed by it. That issue, problem, circumstance or trouble cannot have you; amidst the fire you continue to reflect the image of God. First Corinthians 10:13 says:

*"No temptation has overtaken you except such as is common to man."* Tribulations in the life of a believer should be expected. The reason the bush was not consumed was because God was in it. God did not free Shadrach, Meshach, and Abednego from the fire; instead, He protected them and freed them in the fire. "...it is for your consolation and salvation" (2 Corinthians 1:6). The Holy Spirit has been given to this world to bring conviction of sin, to call sinners to have an encounter with Christ, and to empower the church to live intentionally, to be soul winners, and to witness without fear. Ultimately, the Holy Spirit gives us a clear witness of the person of Jesus. Paul knew that the Holy Spirit was indispensable in order to accomplish all that God had purposed for him to do. Without divine empowering, Paul would not have been able to survive that fierce attack. Without the Spirit's leading and prompting, two-thirds of the New Testament would not have been written and the church would have never been formed. God's ultimate purpose for Paul would have not been fulfilled, which meant that those who were not of Jewish descent (gentiles) would have never heard the gospel. Even though Paul did not understand his future, nor did he know what God's exact plan was for his life, he knew there was a God-given purpose he had to fulfill. Perhaps you do not understand why the devil has attacked you so intensely; why you have had to fight since childhood

to survive, and why death has relentlessly tried to take your life. Maybe you internalize questions such as why have traumas, bad experiences, mental attacks, family, social and financial troubles suddenly come upon you? It's not because God hates you; on the contrary, it's because God will use every negative experience to glorify Himself in you and through you. God uses the worst of our lives, so that we can empathize with those who are going through the same things we have gone through. That is why the Bible refers to you as an open letter. We have been created so that the world can read us and know that we have survived and thrived only by the grace of God! We go through fire, death, tragedies, traumas, but we are still on our feet, trusting in the God who keeps His promises.

Years later, Paul wrote to the church in Rome: "For I consider that the sufferings of this present time are NOT worthy to be compared with the glory which shall be revealed in us" (Romans 8:18). God wants to use you to win others through your tears, battles and pains. Your pain and your struggles are the most powerful factors to win others for Christ because they counteract the message the enemy pitches to the world, which is, "No one understands. You are alone in your pain." Whatever you were delivered from has granted you the divine ability to relate and to deliver others from similar bondages. I am a firm believer that God prepares his delivering army in the valley of defeat. Consider this, when we reach the point where we've been overwhelmed by the struggle, it is at that juncture where we tend to look to God and accept his help. Rest assured, though, the area where you were previously wounded now has greater power and anointing than the other areas of your life. No one can relate, sympathize, or minister to a young girl who is contemplating having an abortion better than the person who has gone through a similar situation; someone who has seen the hand of God bring forgiveness, healing, and restoration to their life.

A diamond, in its original state, is coal. Coal is ugly; it has nothing attractive about it and is dirty. No one puts on a ring or jewelry made of coal. Never has a woman been seen wearing a chain with a coal pendant hanging from her neck. As previously mentioned in this book, for a metamorphic change to occur in the coal to become a diamond, the coal must go through a process: it must endure excessive pressure and heat, and not for a day or for a year, but rather for decades. The process is extensive, meticulous, and requires patience. As it transforms, the coal must maintain its integrity and not crack in the process. If it splits apart during the process, it will never reach its full potential of becoming a diamond. It must endure and maintain its integrity, and not allow the heat and pressure to rob it from being the most precious stone on the planet.

If Paul had fallen apart during the moment of attack, he would have aborted the potential and purpose of his God-given treasure. Years later, he would write in one of his letters: "But we have this treasure in earthen vessels..." (2 Corinthians 4:7). There is no doubt that he understood that his life was a process of formation: from coal to diamond. As you continue reading this book you should ask yourself: How is my spiritual formation coming along? Am I sparkling through the process, or am I wasting the opportunity God has given me to reach my destiny and His plan for my life? God knows that alone we could never carry out His plan. That's the reason why He has given us the antidote, so we don't die because of what we experienced along the way. Remember, God will not allow us to be tempted more than we can resist; but with the temptation He will give us the way of escape. Don't be tempted to give up and throw in the towel. Resist the temptation and take the antidote. Fight, battle, and resist the desires that could disqualify you from later being used with greater strength. If you're going through a situation or deadly attack right now, remember that, although you can't see the venom, this attack is for your consolation and salvation. You will soon be rejoicing and celebrating the outcome of this problem. Despite the mess you endured, the anguish you suffered and the hell you went through, your loss was a sign that restoration was on its way. Your sorrow WILL turn into a rejoicing, your sadness WILL turn into joy, if you endure the process. Don't give up!

## THE PRESENCE OF THE HOLY SPIRIT LIVING IN YOU

The fact that God lives in us makes us the majority. Your finances, race, culture, and physical appearance are irrelevant when God lives inside of you. As stated before, I've never seen someone assaulting a vagabond; thieves usually target people who have something of value. Just like a nice car, expensive jewelry, a fancy watch, luxurious rings, diamond earrings or a pearl necklace, the fact that God's Spirit lives in you makes you a candidate to be attacked by the enemy. He wants to rob you of your God-given fruit of the spirit and the priceless anointing that was deposited in you. The enemy looks for prey that he can ambush, so he can steal what God has purposed for you. Whether God prophesied that you would change the world, become a major blessing to everyone who encounters you, help others reach their optimal purpose, mentor individuals to reach their goals and desires, rest assured the enemy will relentlessly try to disillusion and discourage you in order to impede you from accomplishing what God has already predestined for you to do. When the Holy Spirit lives in you, you have the advantage. The enemy has already been defeated, meaning you are victorious whether you feel like it or not. When the Holy Spirit dwells in you, He keeps you, so you don't become contaminated with the sin of this world.

A fish can live for years in salt water. During its entire life span, it has been immersed in salt water twenty-four hours a day. Interestingly, when you take it out of the water and prepare it in the kitchen, you must add salt to it, so it has flavor. How can that be? During all those years, it lived and swam in salt water, it never became contaminated, even though it was surrounded by salt. It did not become contaminated because its scales, which are its natural defenses, protected its body. The fish's defenses protected it from being con-taminated. So it is with the Spirit who lives in you. He keeps you from becoming contaminated, even though you are surrounded by temptations and vices of sin and spiritual death. When the Holy Spirit lives inside you, He makes you aware of His presence. Many times people have fallen into sin, not because they intention-ally chose to, but rather because people oftentimes forget to access His presence which dwells inside of them. When we become desensitized to sin or play with temptation, the "serpents" abound and we play with fire. That's when the presence of the Holy Spirit is quenched in our consciences. This causes the powerful presence of God to live hidden in our subconscious, and subsequently opens doors in our lives, granting the enemy legal right and access to take dominion over our emotions, thoughts and ultimately our actions.

The church of today has forgotten that the presence of the Holy Spirit dwells in us. This is evident in what we see on television, by the music we listen to, in the lies that come out of our mouths, and in what we allow our eyes to see. Remember the eyes are the windows to the soul. The lack of integrity amongst God's people today is an additional sign that we have not fallen under the conviction of the Holy Spirit, who professedly lives in us. Some years ago, a bracelet that read "What Would Jesus Do?" (WWJD) came out on the retail market. It helped to remind young people of the indwelling presence of Jesus in them; to motivate them to imagine the following: If Jesus was here in this world, what would He do in certain circumstances? The question would help people make decisions according to what Jesus would do. It also served as a reminder of what Jesus would not do if he were in our shoes. What decision would He make? I don't see anything wrong with this; I simply believe we should recognize that our convictions to live right before God without being tainted by sin should originate not just with a bracelet, but in our relationship with the Holy Spirit, who lives in us. The Holy Spirit is not a magic amulet, but someone who lives in every believer to give testimony of Jesus

Christ; to help us in our weaknesses and empower us to be more than conquerors.

Paul knew that the presence of God lived inside him, and so he felt confident and secure; he recognized that God held in His hands the plan for his life. There was no reason to fear or feel insecure. When we discover that the Almighty and All-Powerful God lives in us, that is when we will understand that we were created to be conquerors and overcomers. Failure and defeat are not in God's plan for us. God has programmed us to be overcomers. Jude 24 says: "Now to Him who is able to keep you from stumbling, and to present you fault-less before the presence of His glory with exceeding joy." David said that we are arrows in the hands of the archer. God is aiming us toward the enemy's camp. The arrows were prepared by a process using a hammer and fire.

Your life has been hammered, sharpened, and set on fire, melted and then molded by very unpleasant cir-cumstances. But smile and trust God to uphold you in His hand. He is the Archer. The Archer will not miss. We have been made to tear down the enemy's forces. Trust in God despite what is happening in your life right now. Rest now, because your Archer knows you have been perfected for the mission. What determines that the arrow will reach its target is its resistance against the bowstring. There must be resistance to give strength to shoot the arrow. Do you realize now why the resistance in your life has been necessary? God is preparing to use you to destroy your enemies. Take courage. God has you in His hands, and you will soon see the greatest victory in your life. Resistance is what is going to speed up your journey to victory. It's possible in this very moment that God is tightening the bowstring to develop in us good character, discipline, integrity, and power. He knows when to "shoot" us, but He wants to be sure that in the middle of the journey you do not lose the strength to reach your target. If you lose thrust, you will not reach the goal or the assigned target. It's necessary for God to "pull" us until He is sure we have what is needed to faithfully complete the mission.

## SECURITY AND CONFIDENCE IN GOD IS HIS PLAN FOR MY LIFE

"Those who trust in the LORD are like Mount Zion, which cannot be moved, but abides forever. As the mountains surround Jerusalem, so the LORD surrounds His people from this time forth and forever" (Psalm 125:1–2). You are, in singular or plural form, Mount Zion. We are the church of Jesus Christ. Zion was built upon a rock. Its foundation is firm and permanent. We, the church of Christ, have also been built on the Rock. Mount Zion is so valuable that our security is impenetrable, and the gates of hell will not prevail against it. Those who trust in Jehovah are firmly established on the promises of God. Psalm 125:1 says, "[They] are like Mount Zion." They cannot be removed by the prince of the air, nor by his army or his strategies. Their integrity will not be shaken nor their confidence in God. When we learn to trust in God, He will put mountains around us; giving us the security to think differently. God is our "refuge and strength, a very present help in trouble" (Psalm 46:1). He promises to take care of us. "If He takes care of the birds, He will also take care of you," the poet assures us. And Isaiah 44:2 says that before we were even conceived, God had a plan prepared for us. He will help us fulfill His purposes according to His perfect will. When I think about this important truth, I receive encouragement and courage because I understand that everything I have suffered in my past was, in the end, to prepare me for today. I don't have to ask God why. If I was born poor in a dysfunctional family, suffering abuses, I reflect on the fact that God is with me and surrounds me with His divine protection. This is important in our development, because when someone offends us, mistreats us, or betrays us, it's not to stop us from serving God or to lead us astray, but rather for our consolation and our salvation (2 Corinthians 1:6). Each past or future incident is permitted by God to let us know that God loves us and wants others to experience his love through our story.

# DON'T EXPECT ME TO DIE!

"But after they had looked for a long time and saw no harm come to him, they changed their minds." (Acts 28:6)

In this very moment, the enemy is watching you. He wants to know if you are going to give up or if you are going to continue on this difficult road. "The devil walks about like a roaring lion, seeking whom he may devour" (1 Peter 5:8). Seeking is an interesting word. The Bible teaches us that God looks for worshipers who will worship Him in spirit and truth. "For the eyes of the LORD run to and from throughout the whole earth, [seeking] to show Himself strong on behalf of those whose heart is loyal to Him" (2 Chronicles 16:9, added by author). If we don't recognize this point, we're not going to react correctly. We have an audience watching us. They want to see how we are going to react. Hebrews 12:1 says: "Therefore we also, since we are surrounded by so great a cloud of witnesses, let us lay aside every weight, and the sin which so easily ensnares us, and let us run with endurance the race that is set before us." Surrounded by so great a cloud of witnesses, heaven is watching us, and the angels too. Just as we have a great cloud of witnesses, we also have a great cloud of enemies, spiritual murderers, who in the same way are observing us to condemn us. We are told in Acts 19:15 that the sons of Sceva, wandering exorcists, tried to free a demoniac.

But when they confronted the demon, he told them: "Jesus I know, and Paul I know; but who are you?" I tell you the following with the greatest conviction: Satan is not omnipresent, nor omniscient, nor omnipotent; but he is very astute and shrewd. Paul tells us not to be ignorant concerning the devil's ambushes and traps. The satanic kingdom is strategic and wants you to walk in your flesh. The carnal life interprets every event and trauma the wrong way. The carnal mind observes every trauma, attack, injustice, and abuse, and decides: "No more! It's not worth it. It's not worth the sacrifice or the waste of time."

Doctors say that when a person is about to die, they are released from the earthly to enter the eternal. In the same way, with this book in your hands, you have the power to die now or continue boldly fighting and conquering ground for the Lord. Those who were surrounding Paul on that island waited a long time for the apostle to die. In the same way, the devil waits for you to die as well. I can picture the demons, holding hands, hoping to see Paul's future snuffed out; if the promise concerning him would cease and if the Timothys in the faith would go without a mentor and spiritual father. The enemy not only takes notice of the present, but he also takes regard of every prophetic word spoken over your life, so that he can contend against them. Satan's assignment is that not one word, that has come out of the mouth of God, would come to pass. For this reason, Paul tells Timothy to wage war concerning the promises spoken over his life. There are people you are going to impact. A generation is waiting for the rod of authority. Don't let it fall. Be bold, take dominion and establish His kingdom here on earth!

# DISCUSSION QUESTIONS FOR CHAPTER 7

1.  What was your "antidote"?

2.  What role does the Holy Spirit play in your personal life?

3.  What areas qualify as "fire," and which ones as "pressure", resembling the process coal goes through to become a diamond?

4.  Describe three ways that make you feel that you are in the process of being transformed from a piece of coal into a diamond.

5.  What practical principles can you apply from Jude 24?

6.  What message will you send to your enemies who are waiting for your death?

7.  Just as Paul did with Timothy when he left him his spiritual legacy, can you name a "Timothy" God has put in your life so that, in the same way, you can transfer a legacy to that person?

# CHAPTER 8

# ONLY A SCAR REMAINS

"...for I bear in my body the marks of the Lord Jesus." (Galatians 6:17) When Paul begins his ministry as apostle, pastor, evangelist, teacher, and prophet, he carries with him a reminder of how God had spared him from death: a scar on his hand. With every letter he writes (two-thirds of the New Testament is made up of his thirteen epistles), he undoubtedly reflects on how God has been with him. While he writes from jail, the flames of the candle light up the scar on his hand. The scar—marked by two tiny dots, indented from the fangs of the viper—is a seminary, a message, and a reminder of the plan and mission of God for his life. The powerful message of the scar is "I suffered it, I survived it, and now I have a license to talk about it." When he prayed with his hands raised, he saw the marks that the serpent had left on his hand. This gave him inspiration to keep going forward without caring about what he was experiencing at that moment. He knew that the same God who had healed his painful and bleeding wounds was also going to heal his painful and distressful situation. God would continue being glorified despite the circumstance. As he laid his hands on the sick, each time seeing that scar, he indisputably received more inspiration and faith. When he laid his hands on Timothy (2 Timothy 1:6), he prayed for the anointing to empower him and that he would receive an impartation of tenacity and strength to resist every attack against him. When he laid his hands on the new believers to receive the Holy Spirit, he also prayed that the same Holy Spirit would heal every wound suffered in the journey. When he looked at his hand, the scar transported him back to that unforgettable night (Acts 28:3–6); reminding him of the antidote of the Holy Spirit, who freed him from a sure death. It was impossible for any sickness to resist those rivers of faith that flowed from Paul's life.

In the times in which we live, scars are considered unpleasant and shameful. Those who have these marks try to get rid of them or hide them. They apply all kinds of makeup, creams and even cocoa butter to try to make them disappear. However, our life in Christ is different. The more scars you carry in your body, the more opportunity you will have to honor God for His faithfulness. A scar shows the place where a wound or lesion has been healed. According to The Oxford Dictionary, to heal is "to unite that which has been cut or broken." Jacob was transformed from a usurper and deceiver to a righteous patriarch. God gave him a new name, a new identity, and a new scar. Along with the inheritance of nations God had given him, Jacob received a wound in his thigh that made him limp for the rest of his life. His scar was not a shameful one, but one of honor and gratitude to His God. Every step he took was a reminder of his total dependence on God. This chapter should remain clear in our lives. At times we recite prayers contrary to God's will. We ask Him to make the scars disappear from our lives without understanding that the scar is necessary to bring to pass the destiny God has planned for us. Your prayers will be more fervent, your songs will be more passionate, and your testimony will be more convincing each time you use your scar as a powerful weapon in God.

God wants to heal every wound and hurt in your present life to glorify Himself regarding your past. Your present wound will be your future blessing. You will not have to make excuses or justify your scar, but rather, you will show it to the whole world with courage, confidence, and security. The scar on Paul's hand was a sign of victory! He had a history that the entire world needed to know. Celebrate your scar, because it will be the key that will open doors, cross borders, bring blessings, and resonate with people, making it possible for you to relate to those who are going through the same or even worse situations. Learn to talk about and show that scar with authority and confidence. Remember, the scar is a mark of a healed wound.

The antidote of the Holy Spirit and the balm of the Lord Jesus Christ have freed us from what the devil had planned. The evidence we have of this great victory is our scar. Not all scars are the same; rather, all are different. There are no two alike. They come in different sizes and distinct forms. Some are bigger than others. But all have a story to tell. The one who has tried to conceal it has not discovered the true significance of his scar and is wasting a lifetime trying to hide it. Let us discover the power and purpose of our scar and give glory to God for it. Your pain takes on a new purpose when we begin to understand that our scars are reminders of God's faithfulness. Scars are memoirs of how God allowed us to endure and survive the vicious attack sent to kill us. Paul learned to share his scars and understood they were a powerful weapon:

". . .for I bear in my body the marks [scars] of the Lord Jesus" (Galatians 6:17). Paul never forgot the value of the scars he carried in his body. He always remembered them and made mention of them. He referred to his marks like a good soldier who mentions the medals that have been awarded to him for his excellent military service. He knew that his scars would serve to put into effect the plan and the power of the gospel. However, times have changed and unfortunately scars are not deemed as valuable trophies anymore but as unattractive and embarrassing marks. Our culture would rather hide the scar, along with the story, in hopes of not having to revisit the memory. Advertising today tells us that "image is everything;" that is, "Take care of your image and reputation because that will be the pathway for your future." Men don't cry, and women who do are weak and don't understand their rights. Society says: The more fragmented and messed up you are, the fewer opportunities you will have.

Why is it that suffering, pain, or scars are enemies of this progressive generation? In Galatians 3:3, Paul speaks to the church in a tone of exhortation: "Are you so foolish? Having begun in the Spirit, are you now being made perfect by the flesh?" I believe with all my heart that this same urgent rhetorical question must be answered in order to go to the next level. Paul, as a minister of God, doesn't use a credit card as his credentials; rather, he uses his wounds, sufferings, and scars to prove his ministry. The perspective of this servant was that every scar in his body had a story to tell, with the intent of God's glory being made well-known everywhere. The process that it takes for a wound to become a scar requires time. Each wound is different. The process is painful, frustrating, and hard at times. But the scar, in the end, is a message to the world that God is faithful and His mercy is forever. Don't get frustrated when you see that your scar is taking longer than expected to heal. When the skin is torn, the body forms collagenous fibers (proteins) to fill in the lesion and repair the wound, creating the scar. There is no pre-determined time for the complete healing of that scar. All scars are different. When you suffer an emotional or psychological wound, the balm of prayer, forgiveness, experiences with God, and time itself are the ingredients to repair the wound and heal it. God always reminded the prophets, as well as His people, not to forget from where He had delivered them. The reason for this is that a human being is forgetful about what God does for him. We must never forget from where God delivered us, and how close we were to death; how God, at the right time, heard our cry and intervened to help us. When you begin to doubt and forget what God has promised you, look at your scars. Don't see them as something negative, but as a certificate for graduating from the seminary of "pain, bitterness, and anguish," which are your required credentials to encourage and heal those who are shedding the same tears you used to shed. You will be able to feel compassion for them and be a strong tower so that the world knows that all you have endured and suffered is now just a scar!

# DISCUSSION QUESTIONS FOR CHAPTER 8

1. Describe the most prominent scar of your life.

2. What message does your scar send to the world around you?

3. The powerful message of the scar is: "I _____ it, _____ it, and now I have a _____ to speak about it."

4. Describe the process of the wound, the healing, and the scar.

5. What did you learn from your scar?

6. What is the greatest danger in trying to cover up a scar?

7. The more _____ you carry in your body, the more _____ you will have to honor God for His _____.

# CHAPTER 9

# RESURRECTION POWER

In 1948 Ernest Neal, would write a book that would be considered one of the greatest contributions to the world of mammals, making the badger the only species of the genus Mellivora. Neal's exhaustive work and study would bring national exposure and unveiled the unique characteristics of this foreign but intriguing animal in his book *The Badger,* which showed the first photo of this little creature.

Part of the reason why the badger was discovered so late is because by nature it is a nocturnal animal. From Ireland to Japan, the badger increased in number, but its activities were ignored together with its habits. This mammal is unique in the world. It is known for being loving and caring. Neal frequently says in his book that the badger has been seen adopting litters of skunks when their parents die at the hands of hunters. The badger is known to have a tender heart but tough skin. Their skin is hard to penetrate and its looseness allows them to twist and turn on their attackers when held. The only safe grip on a honey badger is on the back of the neck. Their skin has been known to be impervious to poacher's machetes, spears and in some cases bullets.

There are various classes of badgers but there is one in particular that I would like to allude to and that is the "honey badger." Though docile and humble by nature, in 2002 *National Geographic* recognized it as the fiercest predator that exists. In its 2003 edition, the *Guinness Book of Records* featured the badger as the most fearless animal, not only for its aggressiveness or for how dangerous it is, but also for the inner characteristics it possesses. It is recognized as one of the fiercest animals because it has been seen fighting off lions, leopards and hyenas and in some occasions chasing them off and taking their prey. When in danger a honey badger has been observed putting up a huge display, growling and releasing a scent similar to a skunk.

For years, the cobra was considered the most feared creature of the desert, and the most dangerous in the world. People familiar with the cobra know that whenever it confronts its victim, it raises its head and prepares to inject its deadly venom. If it's a *Mozambique* cobra, it spits in the eyes of its victim to burn the corneas, blinding the victim with venomous toxins before destroying it. Whether it's a lion, gorilla, hyena, or any other animal from the jungle, all of them become victims of the venomous cobra. Although the animal may be dangerous, fierce, or large, it cannot resist the deadly venom of the cobra.

Just as there are many similarities between a honey badger and a disciple of Jesus Christ (relentless, fearless and fierce yet tender hearted, tough-skinned and loving), I noticed resemblances between our adversary Satan and a Mozambique Cobra. The herpetologist C. H. Pope says that "snakes are first cowards, then bluffers, and last of all warriors." They're nocturnal and come in different forms, colors, and sizes. There are 32 species of snakes in eight genuses. Some weigh only eight ounces, while others weigh 320 pounds, reaching a large size of almost 33 feet.

For many years, the Mozambique Cobra was regarded as the fiercest animal. With its acidic spit and highly lethal venom, not to mention it's swift movement and speedy attack, *National Geographic* crowned it the fiercest animal in the kingdom. I recall watching an episode of *National Geographic* in which the "Undisputed Fearless Champion" would face a much smaller yet "Fearless Champion" of his own kind, the honey badger. I remember thinking how can an animal so docile and loving be categorized as number one on the list of National Geographic's most dangerous animals in the world. Even more so than the scorpion, centipede, or the cobra?

While I watched the program intently, I witnessed the battle for "Ferocity Supremacy" between the Cobra Mozambique vs. The Honey Badger. This battle would not only determine desert supremacy it would give the undisputed title to the National Geographic champion. As they confront each other they move side to side while staring at one another. They try to strike at each other, but they dodge each other time after time because of the rapid instincts of both predators. The cobra raises its head and begins to move rapidly, suddenly and with intensity he latches on to his opponent and injects him with deadly venom. The badger backs off, losing its strength. Nevertheless, the dose of deadly venom that now runs through its body is too much, and he can't resist it, ultimately collapsing and eventually dying. I was reminded of the early fights of Mike Tyson where we would all watch in great anticipation... for one minute and then to our surprise the fight is over.

After delivering the fatal blow via it's deadly bite, as is his custom, the cobra pompously begins to circle around its prey, perhaps singing Queen's 1980 hit

"Another One Bites the Dust." For a span of three hours, it circles and parades around the defeated badger. It was too busy caught up in its pretentiously – snobby victory parade to take notice of what will be a wake-up call for the ages. You see, the Cobra does not know that while it's celebrating the defeat of its defenseless victim, something is happening inside the badger's body that is undetectable to even the keenest eye. To understand what is occurring, it is necessary to familiarize yourself with the honey badger's nature. During its whole life, it has been accustomed to plundering honeycombs in order to feed off its honey. Without option, the honey badger goes head to head with bees and is frequently attacked by swarms of them. Often covered by bees from top to bottom and stung thousands of times a week, every sting has prepared him for his ultimate battle. He has been equipped by pain and made venomously immortal by his adversary's frequent and relentless attacks.

While the cobra is celebrating its victory, it doesn't know that the badger, although fallen and unconscious, has created an antibody in its system. The badger, in reality, is not dead. Instead, it is going through a process of regeneration and to some degree resurrection. Its body is creating an antidote to counter the deadly dose it suffered. Soon it opens its eyes, gets up, shakes its head violently, and rushes to defeat the now vulnerable, unarmed snake which failed in its mission to destroy him. Now, in control of all its faculties, the honey badger begins to pursue the cobra who tries to escape but is unsuccessfully. The badger catches up to the defenseless and terrorized cobra and with one bite rips off its head and in the end, devours it. What an upset! Indeed, this was like a Mike Tyson fight. I would assimilate it to one of the greatest upsets in boxing history February 11, 1990 in Tokyo, Japan when Mike Tyson was knocked out by 42-1 underdog Buster Douglas. After the fight, it was discovered that leading up to the match, Douglas faced several setbacks, including the death of his mother, Lula Pearl, 23 days before the fight. Additionally, the mother of his son was facing a severe kidney ailment, and he had contracted the flu on the day before the fight. Yet against all odds Buster Douglas' relentless attack on Mike Tyson set him up for what could easily be regarded as the greatest upset in sports history.

Because God sees the end from the beginning, it is my firm belief that when life is lived according to God's word, every struggle, trouble and tribulation has been permitted to teach us, train us, prepare us and ultimately glorify our Lord and Savior. "And I will put enmity between you and the woman, and between your seed and her Seed; He shall bruise your head, and you shall bruise His heel" (Genesis 3:15). Satan took Christ to the cross with the intention of scoffing and shaming him. When Christ died on the cross, Satan had a great celebration over the death of the Son of God. But on the third day, the Spirit of God resurrected Jesus Christ from the dead, similar to what the badger did to the cobra. He crushed the serpent's head and fulfilled the first prophecy of Genesis 3:15. "O Death, where is your sting? O Hades, where is your victory?" (1 Corinthians 15:55). A new headship has been established! Christ has been exalted and is now the head of the church, the greatest organism on the face of the Earth.

What prepares the badger for encounters with deadly enemies are the previous attacks and bee stings. Although it doesn't understand the why of the pain from the bee stings and attacks, they are indispensable for its growth, development, and destiny. I'm sure that at any given moment we may ask ourselves, "Why me? why my children, why my spouse, why my family, why my finances, why my ministry? Why do the ungodly prosper, and I, a righteous person who fears God, never seem to get ahead?" The psalmist asked himself the same question and concluded that he almost lost his foothold. "But as for me, my feet had almost stumbled; my steps had nearly slipped. For I *was* envious of the boastful, when I saw the prosperity of the wicked" (Psalm 73:2-3). May we never forget the honey badger, an underdog in *its own right. A reminder that though the odds are stacked against him his fearless tenacity give* no room for fear to paralyze it.

My prayer for you is that you never forget the honey badger. While it appeared to have a lower probability of winning the battle against the infamous snake, it was its past battles with bee stings that helped prepare it for its final victory. When you cry and shed tears and fight against the torments of life, don't blame God. It is during these times of torment that there is something occurring inside of you that is much more powerful than the external events. Every attack against you builds up your spiritual antibodies. Every tear strengthens your faith, and every time you are scorned by others, it helps to multiply the antidote in your spiritual cells. "But if the Spirit of Him who raised Jesus from the dead dwells in you, He who raised Christ from the dead will also give life to your mortal bodies through His Spirit who dwells in you" (Romans 8:11). Paul had the Spirit of God as an antidote living inside him. In the same way, he constantly suffered pain and bitterness, which prepared him to fulfill his destiny and God's purposes. I believe that many of us do not know our final destiny, not understanding that the afflictions we are encountering shape us to attain what God has prepared for us. Therefore, let us accept the fights, the tests, and the difficulties with open arms, because if God has allowed it all, it's for our edification and salvation. Never forget friend, every tear, hurt, and pain you have suffered has prepared you for this specific moment. God wants you to know that he entrusted you with a specific assignment that only you can accomplish; therefore, your preparation had to be meticulously designed by Him. What you have suffered has served as your incubator. As a result of your endurance and perseverance, You are now ready to soar just as He has predestined!

# DISCUSSION QUESTIONS FOR CHAPTER 9

1. Point out the similarities between a faithful believer and the honey badger.

2. Can you answer the famous question, "Why me?"

3. What do the venomous bee stings represent?

4. What similarities are there between the fight between the honey badger and the cobra, and the fight between the believer and the enemy?

5. What benefit is produced with every tear you shed?

6. What is the antidote?

7. How has God used this book for your restoration and resurrection?